INSIDE THE SUPERNATURAL

Jean Ritchie is a journalist and writer who has contributed to numerous newspapers and magazines nationally and internationally. She is also the author of *Myra Hindley: Inside the Mind of a Murderess, Topping: Memoirs of the Police Chief in the Moors Murders Case, The Secret World of Cults, With the Greatest Respect*. In the course of researching and writing this book she has travelled all over Britain and Europe.

Inside the Supernatural

AN INVESTIGATION INTO THE PARANORMAL

Jean Ritchie

Fontana
An Imprint of HarperCollins*Publishers*

An Imprint of HarperCollins*Publishers*,
77-85 Fulham Palace Road,
Hammersmith, London W6 8JB

A Fontana Original 1992

9 8 7 6 5 4 3 2 1

A catalogue record for this book
is available from the British Library

ISBN 0 00 637809 9

Set in Sabon

Pictures by Emma Cattell

Printed in Great Britain by
HarperCollinsManufacturing Glasgow

Contents

Introduction

Tell anyone that you are researching a book about the paranormal and they will tell you an anecdote from their own life or one from the experiences of their family and friends. It may be something fairly insignificant: a dream that came true; a strange feeling of a ghostly presence; a clock that, in the words of the song 'stopped, dead, never to go again, when the old man died'. Or it may be a full-scale haunting with clanking chains, footsteps and headless nuns; a disruptive poltergeist that hurled objects around; a vision of a dying relative many miles away.

The majority of people *believe* in the supernatural. Sixty per cent believe it is possible to communicate telepathically; fifty-nine per cent believe that some houses are haunted; fifty-nine per cent believe it is possible to dream the future; forty-five per cent believe in reincarnation and thirty per cent believe that we can receive messages from the dead (statistics from a poll carried out for Channel Four in 1987). The word 'believe' implies that they have faith in the fact that these things are possible. What this book attempts to do is find out what factual basis there is for their belief.

An anecdotal story, the sort everyone seems to be able to tell about things that go bump in the night, has no scientific worth. It cannot be investigated, bottled, analysed or dissected. It's like Samuel Goldwyn's verbal contract: not worth the paper it's written on. Yet over the many months I was researching this book I came to realize that the sum of all this experience has to be worth something. If every family has within its culture a story of this kind, the sheer volume and universality of the material must amount to a matter of substance. Sure, the sceptics will say that man has demonstrated his need for mystery and that supernatural stories cater for this need. But there are easier ways to inject mystery into life: religion, for a start. The paranormal is a subject that invites scorn: many of the people who have confided their personal experiences to me have done so diffidently, and in confidence: 'I've never told anyone this before in case they thought I was mad,' is a fairly common fear.

This is not a book about the assorted unconfirmed experiences of all these people. But it is a book *for* them because it is a book which attempts to explain, in lay person's language, just what is happening in the serious pursuit of the paranormal.

Are we any nearer today to understanding what ghosts are? What causes poltergeists? Why some people come back from mediums feeling that they have been in close commune with their dead loved ones – and others feel that they have been ripped off? Is there such a thing as telepathy – and, if so, why can't we harness it and use it?

Research into the paranormal is regarded with some suspicion by the scientific establishment. One eminent American parapsychologist recently estimated that there are no more than fifty scientists worldwide involved in investigating the supernatural on a full-time basis. Fortunately, to counterbalance this, there are some brilliant part-time investigators (several of them, coincidentally, highly-regarded scientists in their own fields) who give their free time and energy to the subject.

Serious psychical research began here in Britain more than a hundred years ago. Although America hhas thrown more money at the subject over the past fifty years, international researchers still look to Britain for good examples of ghost stories: this is the most haunted country in the world.

It is shortsighted of the scientific community to turn its back on psychical research. In terms of world history, it is not long since we all believed that the earth was flat, that the sun revolved around the earth and condemned as lunatics people who talked of stones falling from the heavens (meteorites). We have learned that these beliefs were wrong.

It takes only the quickest glimpse (which is what this book gives you) into the astonishing discoveries of the 'new' physics to realize that there are, indeed, more things in heaven and earth than are dreamt of in our philosophy. If you can get your brain around ideas of relativity and quantum mechanics – which are now scientifically accepted and verified – how very much easier to foresee the day when extra sensory perception is fully and completely explained. We are no more qualified to reject the possibility of that day coming than we were qualified 500 hundred years ago to call the man who was hit on the head by a meteorite a lunatic.

I have a confession to make. I started research on this book as a dyed-in-the-wool sceptic. I did not believe in the paranormal. I finished writing the book from a different personal perspective. I still maintain a very healthy scepticism about a great deal of so-called 'evidence', but I am now convinced that there are many unexplained and fascinating happenings that do not fit into the regular framework of human life, events that can only be encompassed within the definition of paranormal.

I have been greatly helped in researching this book by many experts, whose brains I have picked unashamedly, and to whom the finished product will no doubt appear superficial. To them I quote Oscar Wilde: 'To be intelligible is to be found out.' I didn't set out to further their expertise; I set out to explain to beginners, like myself, just what a vast and fascinating subject this is. I am more concerned with being intelligible than with being found out.

To give you a taste of what the paranormal is all about, let me quote just one of the stories I was told by an acquaintance when she discovered I was writing a book on the subject.

* * *

Dr Betty Cay is an intelligent, well-educated and eminently sensible grandmother, the widow of a GP, and a retired historical geographer in her seventies. As well as spending her days looking after her two grandchildren while her daughter works, she researches and writes local history books, concentrating on areas of her home town, Edinburgh.

Early in 1991 she was trying to put together a book on Saughton, in south-west Edinburgh, and she was running up against a big brick wall. She could not find any information on one crucial small area. She knew that a certain house, known as Sauchton Cottage, was the key to this area. The house, not an impressive manse but an artisan's dwelling, had been the first to be built in the area, at some time during the eighteenth century. The history of the house and the land that originally surrounded it was fundamental to the history of the development of the area.

'Because I was looking after the children and running a home for the family, I measured the amount of time I had for research in the odd couple of hours I could squeeze in each day. I was very keen to get on with the book, but I was completely held up by the lack of information I had about this house.

'I could trace its history back to the latter part of the nineteenth century, but I knew that it went back another hundred years or more and I had no clue as to who had owned it or what land was entailed to it then. If it had been a big, important house, no doubt records would have been kept. But I could find nothing on it.

'The present occupant of the house was as helpful as possible, and arranged for me to visit his solicitor to see the deeds of the property. But I was told by both him and the solicitor that the paperwork only went back to the start of the twentieth century and I had already got most of that information from other sources.

'Nevertheless, I went along. The lawyer gave me an empty room to work in and presented me with a typical bundle of legal documents, tied around with red ribbon. On the top was an inventory of all the documents in the pile. I started to work my way through them, taking notes as I went. The papers were in chronological order.

'Astonishingly, as I progressed, I turned over a document and found underneath it one that dated back to the very beginning of the house in the eighteenth century. It gave the name of the owner of the house and details of his two wives. (He had apparently remarried after his first wife died.) It also gave the name of another woman, who I took to be his third wife.'

The document Dr Cay saw, and from which she made notes, was a 'memorandum on a feu charter': a feu charter being an old Scottish term for a conveyancing deed. Dr Cay was able to get all the details she needed about the early days of the house from the document. With it was another eighteenth-century document that was not relevant and did not help her at all.

She continued with her note-taking, moving on to the much more recent documents which covered the early years of this century. Eventually, constrained by lack of time, she re-bundled the documents in the order in which she had found them, noting from the inventory on the front that her eighteenth-century documents were listed, out of chronology, at the end of all the others. She told the solicitor that she would like to return again the following day to do some more research, and the bundle of papers was left out on the desk for her to resume her research.

The next day she was shocked to find that the eighteenth-century documents were no longer in the pile. What's more, they were not included on the inventory. Upset, Dr Cay called the lawyer, who was in another office. The lawyer insisted that there had never been any eighteenth-century paperwork in the bundle, that there were no papers missing, and that, as Dr Cay had originally been told, it was only possible to trace back ownership of the house through the deeds to the beginning of the twentieth century.

Perplexed, Dr Cay was inclined to wonder whether she had hallucinated the existence of the documents. But she knew she had handled them and read them and she had the evidence of her own notebook in which she had copied out details from them.

Taking the names of the owner and his wives that she had copied from the document, she was able to trace them at Edinburgh's Register House in the official births, marriages and deaths registers. (Scotland was more efficient than England at starting and keeping good records.) Without the initial input of the names from the 'non-existent' document, she would have had no way of knowing where to start. She was able ultimately to find out that the woman she thought was the original owner's third wife was, in fact, the woman to whom he sold the house.

'Eventually, everything slotted into place and I was able to trace the early years of the property. Yet the document I used did not exist! Without having seen it, I could have spent years floundering through records and still never have come up with the information I needed.'

Dr Cay has no explanation to offer for her experience. She believes she may have hallucinated when she saw the documents listed on the inventory, but she is certain that the documents themselves were real enough.

Were they hallucinations? Did she already have the information buried somewhere in her subconscious mind (this is highly unlikely, considering the particular and precise nature of the information involved)? Was her mind in some way tuning in to another source of the material? Was her need (she was desperately short of time for her research) a factor in helping her 'find' the information? If so, why was there also another, irrelevant, document among the bundle?

There are no easy answers to these question or to most of those posed by the paranormal. But there is no shortage of questions. While this book cannot attempt to ask them all, it looks at some of the main ones, and the work that is going on to try to come up with some of the answers.

1
The Search Begins

What have Prime Minister Gladstone, Lord Tennyson, Mark Twain, Sigmund Freud and Aldous Huxley got in common? The answer is that they were all members of the Society for Psychical Research, a pioneering and highly-respected body set up in London in 1882 with the aim of investigating paranormal phenomena 'without prejudice or prepossession of any kind, and in the same spirit of exact and unimpassioned inquiry which has enabled Science to solve so many problems, once not less obscure nor less hotly debated'.

The Society was born out of the general disquiet at the end of the nineteenth century about the nature of the universe. This was before science had taken its quantum leap into the twentieth century, and the prevailing wisdom was that we lived in a mechanical world in which everything – every action and reaction – could be scientifically explained. Charles Darwin's theories of evolution had only added to the feeling of being very tiny cogs in a huge well-oiled machine. But the idea that human beings were not the specially-designed central focus of all creation and were simply highly-evolved monkeys, the 'animals with the big brain', took a lot of getting used to. There was an undercurrent of belief that this could not be all.

Religion offered some solutions, but the intellectuals of the age did not want to reject the discoveries of the modern scientific world in favour of blind faith. They wanted proof which would demonstrate that man was more than just a sophisticated machine and which would measure up to the new scientific standards. The raw material for that proof seemed to exist: there was no shortage of ghost stories; the ability to communicate with the spirits of the dead – accepted from time immemorial in some cultures – had gone from being a popular craze in the middle of the nineteenth century to being the basis for the Spiritualist religion. 'Mesmerism', known today as hypnotism, was beginning to be explored and experiments with telepathy – the linking of two minds without any ostensible means of communication – were being carried out in France.

Perhaps the greatest impetus to investigation was D.D. Home. Today Home is still regarded by many as the most sensational physical medium of all time. Born in 1833 in Edinburgh, taken to America at the age of nine by an aunt, Daniel Dunglas Home was only thirteen when he announced that he was in communication with the spirits of the dead. He became a medium, and rappings and table levitations were common at his seances. Home even appeared to be able to levitate himself, in front of witnesses. He could make objects move around the room, make an accordion play music without touching it, put his head into a burning fire without being singed, and stretch his body, adding as much as six inches to his height while observers held on to him.

Mediums and seances were fashionable at the time, but what distinguished Home from the others – many of whom were undoubtedly frauds extracting easy money from gullible clients – was that he was prepared to work in bright well-lit conditions, and he invited the most sceptical of observers to attend his seances. (Many mediums use the excuse that a sceptic in their midst inhibits their powers.)

He was submitted to fairly rigorous testing. Sir William Crookes, a distinguished physicist and Fellow of the Royal Society, carried out stringent tests, often in the presence of other scientists. Obviously, in the nineteenth century various techniques used by conjurors and frauds today were not understood. None the less, Crookes was not gullible, nor were his peers, and it would be wrong to discredit the witnesses who vouched for Home simply because they belonged to another century. Home did have his critics, among them the poet Robert Browning who disliked the fact that his wife Elizabeth Barrett Browning was a fan of Home. However, in all his long career as a medium, Home was never seriously accused of fraud, and was never caught cheating. Since his death in 1886 there have been many attempts to explain away his feats, the most popular suggestion being that he was an accomplished hypnotist who suggested to his audience that they had witnessed things that never actually happened.

Home lived so long ago, and the eyewitness accounts are so incomplete, that it is impossible to begin to assess the truth. What is certain is that he impressed some distinguished people who, like Crookes, felt that such things should be investigated scientifically and methodically. The Society for Psychical Research was founded by such people, and it attracted the support of some of the most respected scientists, philosophers, politicians and literary figures of the day. Instead of regarding psychical research as a rather suspect pseudo-science, as many people do today, they acclaimed it as an important and developing area. Gladstone said, 'It is the most important work that is being done in the world – by far the most important.'

The SPR was not the first group to examine the paranormal. The history of Christianity is littered with attempts to appraise objectively miracles and miracle workers. Before the rise of spiritualism religious visions were the most common form of supernatural manifestation in Europe and the New World. Some religions are more comfortable with them than others and accept the existence of seers, shamans, wise ones, yogis.

In the secular world, long before the SPR was dreamed of, attempts had been made to test some areas of the paranormal scientifically. At the court of Queen Elizabeth I the mathematician John Dee tried to find hidden objects by using dowsing. Half a century later, Sir Francis Bacon devised some experiments to test the existence of second sight, as it was called, using cards. His controls were good and the experiments were well thought out: they did not differ greatly from those that were used three hundred years later when serious research began.

In France during the reign of Louis XVI, there was a lot of interest in mesmerism, the forerunner of hypnotism, which took its name from Franz Mesmer, a medical student who discovered he could induce trance states in volunteers. He believed the source of the power was magnetism. During the nineteenth century, experiments with hypnotism were carried out, and by the last quarter of the century its existence was accepted even by the most critical scientists.

Spiritualism took on the status of a religion in the 1840s. Spiritualist beliefs have been around since ancient civilization, but they were formalized into a religion after a whole rash of paranormal events made some people believe that they were in touch with the personalities of the dead. There was a fashionable craze for 'table turning', the forerunner of seances, when groups of people in homes all over Europe and America would sit around tables which tilted, turned and even in some instances floated in the air. Queen Victoria and Prince Albert were among those who were confounded by the antics of a table. There was probably a great deal of faking going on, but the scientists who investigated the phenomena were unable to prove that it was all fraudulent. Michael Faraday, the physicist, took the line that 'quasi involuntary' muscle movements of the sitters were causing the effect without them knowing they were doing it, but many of those who were present when tables and chairs floated around rooms refused to accept this explanation. The fashion for table turning died out, though, mainly because, as with all psi, the phenomena are unpredictable. (Psi is a term now used to cover all paranormal experiences, although it was originally intended to link together ESP and PK.) For every exciting experience, there were many boring evenings passed sitting around tables which remained resolutely rooted to the ground. However, for some people the idea of communication with the dead became the foundation of their religious beliefs and Spiritualist churches sprang up across America and Britain.

. The Fox sisters in America were credited with getting spiritualism properly off the ground. In 1848, Margaret and Kate Fox, aged fourteen and twelve, began to 'communicate' with the spirits of the dead by a series of rappings that they heard in their home in New York state. The house was reputed to be haunted, and the Fox family complained of strange banging noises. One night the girls tried snapping their fingers to imitate the noise; every time they did so, the rappings mimicked them. Eventually they started to ask questions and dictate a code to the unknown source of the noise, and they got replies that led them to believe they were in communication with the spirits of the dead.

The events in the Fox household were witnessed by many people, starting with neighbours and friends but eventually spreading to the public at large when the press latched on to them. Their stories were not accepted without questions: commissions were set up to investigate them, and they were paraded before panels of experts. The most common explanation offered for the rappings which the sisters seemed able to produce at will was that they were voluntarily able to dislocate their knee joints and make popping noises with them. If this was true, no one has been able to replicate these noises and nobody has explained how the sisters could fill large meeting halls with sound by this means.

The Fox sisters' strange talents, whether psychic or physical, did not do them any favours. They were marketed by the famous showman, P.T. Barnum, and became nothing more than a music hall act; they were alcoholics, their marriages failed and eventually one of them confessed that they had been cheating all along. Later she denied this, saying that she had made the admission for money. (They were both living in reduced circumstances.) By then, whatever powers they had had waned. The sisters died amid controversy.

Despite this, the Fox sisters' initial success (and no one

has satisfactorily explained how, by knee-popping, they were able to answer so many of the questions put to them by believers and sceptics alike, unless they were able to accumulate information from some non-normal source) spawned a great interest in communication with the dead. Within a few years there were hundreds of mediums across America and Europe who claimed to be able to contact the spirit world.

There were other attempts to set up societies to bring together all those interested in research into the paranormal, and other countries have their own groups. The Parapsychological Association, an international body founded in 1951, is made up of professionals working in the field of parapsychology and has, for scientific reasons, a rather narrower remit than the SPR, though it is more rigorously academic. However, the British SPR remains the most distinguished body of lay people involved in psychic research, even though this research is no longer fashionable, nor as likely to attract as many mainstream scientists as it did in its early years.

After its inception in 1882 the Society divided itself into six different committees, each with a specific area to investigate: thought transference (we call it telepathy today, a word coined in the first year of the Society's existence by one of its founder members, F.W.H. Myers); mesmerism (hypnotism); Reichenbach phenomena (Baron Carl von Reichenbach, the chemist who discovered creosote and paraffin, believed he had also discovered auras of light created magnetically and given off by all organic matter including human beings); apparitions and haunted houses; physical phenomena; and a literary committee to review and research already-published information about psychic phenomena.

The members were an enthusiastic and hardworking bunch. All the committees (with the exception of the one investigating physical phenomena, which found mediums like Home who could create physical effects in the seance room rather thin on the ground) produced lengthy and detailed reports, and threw themselves with great energy into the time-consuming business of carrying out investigations.

Although it is possible today to snipe at some of the Society's early investigative efforts, it is important to remember they were breaking new ground and their techniques improved with practice. It took time to come up with all the controls necessary, to work out all (or even most) of the possible sources of fraud, and to even begin to understand the ways in which they themselves might have been unintentionally influenced to see what was not really there.

Yet they were certainly not easily convinced, and they were more than ready to denounce trickery whenever they found it. There was a serious financial motive for mediums and others to be fraudulent just as there still is today a substantial market in bringing 'messages from the spirit world' to the bereaved. Then, there was also the possibility of stage fame, and even rich patronage.

One of the most notable exposés in the SPR's early days was the famous Madame Blavatsky. Helena Petrovna Blavatsky was a New York immigrant who founded the Theosophical Society in 1875, riding the crest of the wave of interest in spiritualism and attracting as many as one hundred thousand members. Madame Blavatsky claimed to get spirit guidance from a group of 'Mahatmas' in Tibet and that letters from them were 'teleported' to her. When she visited London the SPR set up a committee to investigate her. They tackled the job thoroughly, interviewing witnesses who had seen her physical phenomena and even sending a member to India, to the headquarters of her flourishing movement. Their conclusion, published in 1885, was that 'she has achieved a title to permanent remembrance as one of the most accomplished, ingenious and interesting impostors in history'. The Theosophical Society went into decline.

One of the most vigilant and dedicated of researchers was Mrs Eleanor Sidgwick, wife of the first president of the Society, Sir Henry Sidgwick. She denounced a very popular and acclaimed medium, William Eglinton, who produced spirit messages by slate writing. This was a fashionable method of spiritual communication at the end of the last century, and involved holding a slate on the underside of a table. Scratching noises were heard while the 'spirit' wrote on the slate, and then the message was produced for all to see. To this day, there are those who believe that Eglinton was genuine: but Mrs Sidgwick described his work as 'clever conjuring'.

Eglinton inspired researchers to approach their problem from a different angle by perfecting the methods that are used by the fraudsters in an attempt to see how people can be deceived (a tradition carried on today by the professional sceptics as well as by many parapsychologists). One member of the SPR taught himself to produce slate writing as convincingly as Eglinton and then put his conjuring skills to the test by trying it out on witnesses who were told that he was a medium. Nobody detected his tricks, despite the fact that they were not scrupulously hidden, opening up a whole area of research into how and why our eyes deceive us into seeing what we want to believe. The Society's researchers were so tough that some members felt they went too far. The poet W.B. Yeats commented: 'It's my belief that if you psychical researchers had been about when God Almighty was creating the world, He couldn't have done the job.'

Of course, the researchers' enthusiasm didn't mean they were guaranteed to spot fraud. In the early days of the Society, for example, the Creery sisters were believed to be a first-class example of telepathy. Four sisters and a maidservant from their household were able to detect playing cards, names or objects that had been chosen by independent observers while they were out of the room. Their success rate was remarkably high, and Sir William Barrett, an eminent physicist, was very impressed. But they were later caught out cheating, sending messages to each other in code. They admitted it, and claimed that they had done it before, but only rarely. Whether this admission negated everything that they had previously done, or whether, like many mediums or clairvoyants, they found their powers waning and yet felt compelled to produce results, is arguable and is a moot point with other psychics.

Although scepticism was a prized characteristic of these pioneering psychic researchers, they found plenty to reinforce the original enthusiasm that had led to them setting up the SPR. Richard Hodgson (the man who investigated and exposed Madame Blavatsky) emigrated to America, and there encountered a medium called Mrs Leonora Piper. Mrs Piper would go into a trance and then be taken over by her 'control', Dr Phinuit, who she claimed had been a French physician. In the trance she was able to give information about those sitting with her. Hodgson, sceptical, assigned a private detective to watch her and her husband to find out how they were researching the information, which she was passing off as obtained from the spirits of the dead. He reluctantly accepted that there was no 'normal' way in which Mrs Piper could know many of the things she did. No trace was ever found of Dr Phinuit's existence in historical records, nor could he speak any French. This is not unusual with mediums, whose 'controls' are thought to be secondary personalities of their own rather than real historical people (see chapter 5). However, after one of Hodgson's own friends, George Pelham, died, he took over as Mrs Piper's control and Hodgson was provided with a large amount of bafflingly accurate information from his own life. Mrs Piper described a young woman who had died in Australia and to whom Hodgson had been very close – including a description of a birthmark which was a strange spot of blue colour in an otherwise brown eye. On one occasion Hodgson brought a friend with him whom 'Pelham' seemed not to recognize, but when told the woman's name 'Pelham' replied that she was 'the little girl, now grown up' which was accurate because Pelham had known her as a child.

Although Hodgson scrupulously recorded the details at the time, we can never be sure a century later how much of the 'proof' for a medium like Mrs Piper is merely anecdotal and subjective. However, Hodgson was certainly not the only cynical researcher to be impressed by Mrs Piper. When she visited England she was investigated by a distinguished group, including F.W.H. Myers, a leading member of the SPR, and Sir Oliver Lodge, the physicist. They took extreme precautions to make sure that she did not meet any of the people who would attend her seances beforehand, and she gave them permission to intercept and monitor all her letters. They, too, were finally unable to explain how she obtained her information unless it was by paranormal abilities. What was not clear – then or now – was whether she was, as she claimed, in touch with the spirits of the dead, or whether she was using highly-developed telepathy to garner knowledge from the individuals who sat with her. She continued to practise as a medium for twenty-five years, and was never discovered acting fraudulently.

Mrs Piper became a celebrated public figure and this encouraged other women to test their own mediumistic abilities. Mrs Margaret Verrall, a Cambridge scholar, showed that she, too, had some exceptional talents. So did a medium who called herself 'Mrs Holland', but who was really Mrs Fleming, sister of Rudyard Kipling. Interestingly, comparisons of the automatic writing of these women (in a trance they would appear to take dictation from their control) revealed quite a few cross-correspondences in the information they gave, as though one was confirming the messages of another, even though it was impossible for them to be in collusion: Mrs Verrall lived in Cambridge and Mrs Fleming in India.

An Italian peasant woman, Eusapia Palladino, gave the early researchers their best opportunity to study a medium who could produce physical effects similar to those produced by D.D. Home. Palladino appeared to be able to levitate tables, move objects around, nudge or pinch sitters who were outside her arms' reach. Sitters claimed they could actually see her developing extra arms and limbs during seances. Marie Curie and her husband Pierre were among the many scientists who, over a thirty-year period, were astonished by her apparent abilities.

Palladino did not shy away from investigation, and she was prepared to work in good light so that those who were watching her could clearly record what went on. Although one early report from the SPR accused her of fraud, a later and more detailed one found that she was capable of producing astonishing phenomena. There is no doubt that she cheated from time to time, but her defenders say that when she was in a trance she had no control of herself and it was up to the investigators to hold tight to her hands and legs to prevent her movement. On one occasion, she even cried out to them to hold her more tightly or she would cheat.

As she grew older and her powers waned she resorted to cheating more. It is hard to condemn a simple peasant who had been catapulted to international celebrity for wanting to perpetuate her failing skills, but unfortunately her predilection for cheating cast a cloud over all her other achievements.

Some researchers believe that anyone who has been caught in any fraud should automatically be discounted from serious research for ever. Others believe (with some evidence from modern laboratory parapsychology to support them) that cheating can facilitate real phenomena, almost as though the mediums have to get themselves in the mood by practising artificially what they want to happen by paranormal means.

Perhaps the greatest of the early mental mediums (as distinct from a physical medium like Palladino) was Mrs Gladys Osborne Leonard, who was the best in the field in the years between the Wars. A Londoner, she first came to the attention of the SPR when she 'communicated' with Sir Oliver Lodge's son Raymond, who was killed in the First World War. She, too, seems to have been beyond suspicion of fraud. The SPR again assigned a private detective to investigate her life, without finding anything that suggested she was researching information. She put herself at the disposal of the SPR for investigation and was paid a retainer by them to be always available for testing. To eliminate the possibility of telepathy, many of her sittings were attended by 'proxies', people standing in for those for whom she was asked to get information from the spirit world. Often the proxies knew nothing more than the name of the person they represented, so there was no possibility of Mrs Leonard being able to extract clues from them by telepathy.

The SPR was not concerned only with investigating mediums. In the early days the literary committee took on the formidable task of collecting and publishing a massive chronicle of spontaneous paranormal experiences which they gathered by appealing in the press. They checked out all the cases they published (before telephones were commonplace and when travelling around Britain took days, this in itself was a formidable achievement) and in 1886 published *Phantasms of the Living, 701 cases of apparitions and crisis visions.* Eight years later they brought out the *Census of Hallucinations*, another massive tome. Both books are still quoted as reliable source material.

These records were, inevitably, largely anecdotal and subjective, although the SPR did check each case for corroboration. Some Society members were already aware of the need for controlled experiments that could be monitored, verified and repeated, a need that has bedevilled psychical research ever since. As early as 1889, telepathy tests were carried out under stringent conditions, the results obtained measured against those they would expect to find by chance. Consistent with subsequent experience, they found some people who could score above chance, and many others who could not.

This kind of experimentation went on the back burner, though, for nearly twenty years until Professor Gilbert Murray, a Professor of Greek at Oxford University, revived interest. He played a parlour game with his family in which he would go out of the room and then try to 'guess' targets that they set for him. Murray fared better when the target set was a scene containing some action and some emotion than when it was a simple object or word. His experience has since been corroborated by recent experiments by parapsychologists like Charles Honorton doing ganzfeld work (see chapter 3). Murray was also unusual in that the whole family, friends and witnesses would try to 'send' the picture to him – most telepathy experiments involve only one sender.

Some of his results were remarkable. When the target was 'Jane Eyre at school, standing on a chair and being called a liar by Mr Brocklehurst', Murray came up with: 'My mother being at a French school ... I reject that. But a sense of obloquy. Girl standing up on a form in a school ... a thing in a book, certainly. I think they are calling her a liar.'

When the subject was the sinking of the *Lusitania* he got it straight off. 'I've got this violently. I've got an awful impression of naval disaster. I should think it was the torpedoing of the *Lusitania*.'

For a time even Murray himself thought that he might be getting clues to his targets through his extremely good hearing, but he was not consciously aware of hearing the targets being discussed. He certainly fared better when they had been discussed than when a target was simply written down, although this did not completely hamper him. Sometimes he picked up things that were in the minds of the senders, but which they had neither spoken nor committed to paper. For example, when his daughter set him a target of a scene from a Russian book in which some children were being taken to see their grandparents, he came up with the information that they were taken across the River Volga. He had never read the book, nor was the river mentioned when the target was discussed, but in fact he was correct: the book did describe the children being taken across the Volga.

In the 1920s, more and more research time was given over to laboratory-type experiments, with tests for clairvoyance and telepathy through guessing cards. But, by then, this type of research was taken more seriously in America, where universities were getting in on the action and academics were being given funding to study the paranormal full-time (unlike the SPR volunteers).

In the 1930s the work of J.B. Rhine, the founding father of modern parapsychology, firmly established academic interest in the subject. It was Rhine who coined the word 'parapsychology' and also 'ESP', or extra sensory perception, an umbrella term covering telepathy, clairvoyance and all other forms of paranormal communication.

Rhine was first attracted to the subject after hearing Sir Arthur Conan Doyle, the creator of Sherlock Holmes and a dedicated spiritualist, give a talk in Chicago. It sparked an interest in him and his wife Louisa – another great contributor to psychic research – that would last a lifetime. But after an unhappy encounter with a celebrated medium, who they both deemed to be a fraud, the Rhines were convinced that the way forward was through systematic and academically credible research. While working at Duke University in Durham, North Carolina, in the late 1920s and early 1930s, Rhine professionalized the subject by introducing statistics. Although earlier work had been done with 'guinea pigs' who claimed no specific psi abilities, most research had centred on people who claimed or appeared to have specific talents. It was Rhine who initiated large-scale testing of ordinary individuals, and made sure that all his results were compared with those he might have expected to obtain by chance: a protocol that has been adhered to by parapsychologists ever since.

Rhine refined the standard card-guessing games by having a colleague, Karl Zener, devise a new set of five cards, each featuring a simple symbol: star, plus-sign, circle, rectangle, wavy line. These cards, made into packs of twenty-five with five of each, are known as Zener cards. The idea behind them was to get away from the emotive connotations of playing cards, and also to give very clearly individual symbols for 'guinea pigs' to try to 'pick up'.

Testing students at random, Rhine soon found several individuals who demonstrated unusual psi abilities. He was able to test them and find consistent patterns: they performed less well when they were tired, they performed less well on certain drugs. He and his fellow researchers devised experiments that distinguished between telepathy and clairvoyance.

It was the publication of Rhine's book, *Extra Sensory Perception*, in 1934, that put parapsychology on the map. By and large, Rhine's methodical approach and statistical rectitude confounded them. The book and its sequel became popular with mass-circulation newspapers and magazines and national radio stations queuing to interview Rhine. The orthodox psychologists (themselves still pioneering a new discipline) gave grudging approval to Rhine's work.

He was not entirely above criticism although (luckily for the growing band of parapsychologists encouraged by the acceptance of his work) none of the research with which he was associated was seriously discredited until 1978. Even then, it was not Rhine himself who was accused of distorting statistics, but a British mathematician, S.G. Soal, who had tested a great deal of people with a card-guessing experiment in the 1940s. Only when he looked at their results for 'temporal displacement' did he find two of them were scoring well above chance. Temporal displacement means that although they were not necessarily getting the right card each time, they were accurately predicting the following card or a preceding card. (In the case of Soal's examples they were both guessing the card to come, but that need not have been the case.)

Soal was accused of falsifying his results, and Rhine was implicated because his Parapsychology Laboratory at Duke University checked and approved some of Soal's research. Thirty years later a computer expert scrutinized Soal's research and confirmed that 'the sad and inescapable conclusion remains that all the experimental series in card-guessing carried out by Dr Soal must, as the evidence stands, be discredited'. Rhine, though not colluding, had been economical with the truth when publishing conclusions that seemed to authenticate Soal's work.

The Soal scandal is one of relatively few accusations of straightforward cheating that have been levelled at psychical researchers and parapsychologists, although they have regularly been accused of being duped or of misinterpreting data (see chapter 7). In general, the early members of the Society for Psychical Research and the pioneers of laboratory work inspired by Rhine set high standards for those who came after them.

2

Things That Go Bump in the Night

Pete the Polt is an obliging sort of ghost who believes in paying his way: he materializes five-pound notes for the people he is haunting. Crumpled fivers arrive out of thin air. They turn up pinned to the ceiling; wedged between the blades of machinery; one even appeared in the open air and fluttered to the ground at the feet of the man of whom Pete seems to be particularly fond. This man also found a ten-pound note on the window of his car. Altogether, about ninety pounds have appeared, as well as several one-pound coins and handfuls of pennies.

Pete the Poltergeist has been making his presence felt for the last six years – not always in such a benign way. His 'home' is a small lawnmower repair workshop, with a hardware shop in front, in the Cathays district of Cardiff.

The business is owned by John Matthews and his wife, Pat. They are helped out by Pat's brother, Fred Cook, and his wife, Gerry. Fred seems to be Pete's particular favourite, but all four of them have seen plenty of evidence of Pete's existence. So, too, have several other people: neighbouring shopkeepers, salesmen visiting the business, customers and other staff who have worked there over the years.

Most impressively, Dr David Fontana, a lecturer in educational psychology at Cardiff University, who was deputed by the Society for Psychical Research to investigate Pete, has been able to witness phenomena occurring. On one occasion, he was accompanied by a colleague from the university when Pete was demonstrating his prowess as a stone thrower.

17

It was stone throwing that first alerted John Matthews to his uninvited guest. The business was then being run from a single-storey building in the yard at the back of the shop and workshop. At that time, John had a partner, Graham, and both men were constantly irritated by the sound of stones hitting the corrugated roof. They assumed it was vandals and reported it to the police more than once. The police investigated and found nothing.

When the business transferred to the bigger premises, the stone throwing increased – but this time it was inside. As John, Graham and a young lad who worked for them, Richard, were busy repairing lawnmowers, they would hear small stones striking the walls all around them and dropping to the workbenches and the floor. Originally, they suspected each other.

'So one afternoon after we'd locked the shop and there was nobody else around, we all put our hands on the counter so that none of us could cheat. And the stone throwing continued,' said John, a down-to-earth Welshman in his fifties who had never even heard the word poltergeist at this stage.

'After a bit, Richard said we ought to write down what was happening. As soon as he spoke a pen plopped down on the counter. So then he started asking for things. He said, "Bring us a plug. Bring us the big end off a mower." All sorts of things. As he asked for them, they arrived. I couldn't have found them that fast myself in the workshop. That's when we knew it was something intelligent.'

Since then, both Graham and Richard have left, though not because of Pete. Pat has started to work more in the shop and her brother and sister-in-law, Fred and Gerry, are also both there most days. There have been other part-time employees, all of whom have seen and heard Pete.

'At first Richard seemed to be his favourite, but now it is Fred,' said John. 'It does more for Fred than anyone. It was when Fred said, "Why don't you bring us something useful, Pete," that the money started coming.'

But the money is a relatively recent development, and has coincided with Pete getting altogether quieter. For a long time, John, his colleagues, and anyone else who was there – including Dr Fontana – were able to have throwing games with Pete, aiming small stones into the most active corner of the workshop (the area where most of Pete's phenomena occurred) and having stones thrown back instantaneously. By marking the ones they threw they could check that they were not getting the same ones back and, after experimenting with rebounds and different trajectories, David Fontana was satisfied that there was no natural explanation for the stones.

Other phenomena have included bolts materializing in mid air, cutlery being taken out of drawers and spread on the table (almost as though Pete was trying to lay the table), cutlery being bent, paper and paperclips materializing to order (the paper often seemed to have come from the offices above the shop, where an accountant has his business). Distinctive teaspoons from a restaurant a few doors away have also turned up on the staircase at Fred and Gerry's home. On one occasion, Pat challenged Pete to produce a dirty paintbrush and one which was not one of their own arrived at her feet.

Pete seems to be fascinated by the carburettor floats which John uses in his business. These are small rubber floats pierced by a sharp metal pin, which allows them to be stuck into different surfaces. They have been found sticking from the ceiling of the workshop. When Pat asked for money, she found a float holding a crumpled five-pound note on to the ceiling. They have appeared in all sorts of odd places in the workshop and, most surprising of all to John and Fred, they have turned up away from the business premises, usually at Fred and Gerry's house.

'On one occasion we left one on top of the heater in the workshop when we locked up at night, challenging it to move. As we drove home, Fred went to buy some fags and when he scooped up his change off the shop counter, there was a float with it,' said John.

On another occasion, Fred thought he had been stung by a wasp because he felt a sharp prick under his shirt but, when he undid his buttons, he found a carburettor float pinned to him. And once, when Fred, Pat and Gerry were sitting under a sun umbrella in Fred and Gerry's garden, all three of them saw the pin from a float pierce the canvas umbrella. John and his family are a pragmatic, easy-going group, none of whom have had any previous interest in or experience of psychic matters. Both couples, John and Pat, and Fred and Gerry, are in their fifties, with grown-up families. They have accepted the presence of Pete the Polt in much the same way that they accept any new arrivals in the business – everyone is made to feel welcome. They have even become fond of Pete, and Fred described the experience of encountering such an active poltergeist as 'a privilege'. But not everything about the experience has been happy. There have been one or two narrow escapes. For instance, when a large bolt of wood was hurled across the workshop and when metal stepladders were thrown across the shop, breaking some of the plates that were on sale. Seed and fertilizer, which is sold in the shop, has frequently been scattered all over the floor and the counter when they have arrived at work in the morning and, on one occasion, fertilizer was thrown over a customer. When Pat is in the toilet she is upset to find stones being thrown around her while the door is locked.

'I don't like the idea of him being in there with me,' she said. Although she does not mind when Pete fingers and plays with her hair.

Other phenomena have worried the family because of the risks. The poltergeist has seemed able to create fire and once they arrived at work to find the engine of a giant lawnmower had been started and left running, emitting dangerous fumes. This happened on a Monday morning, so there was no possibility that the mower had been left on by them: it would have run out of petrol over the weekend. Only a strong man could have started the difficult engine, from which a spark plug had been removed for safety.

'That worried me a bit. If it could start that engine and put back a spark plug that we had removed, what couldn't it do?' said John.

Fred, who was originally very fond of Pete, has had the

most alarming experiences, and now tries to discourage the whole affair, ignoring new phenomena. On four occasions he has seen an apparition in the workshop, the figure of a small schoolboy, aged about nine or ten, but dressed in the sort of clothing worn in the 1940s and 1950s – a school cap, grey shorts, heavy shoes. Once, the apparition was sitting on the handle of a lawnmower, swinging its legs; once on the shop till; and once on a set of shelves in the 'active' corner. Fred could not make out a face or hands and the apparition seemed not to be limited by the physical shape of the room because when it was sitting on the top shelf in the workshop half of its body should, logically, have stuck through the ceiling. Although John was with Fred during at least one of these sightings, John could see nothing.

When Fred saw the apparition for the fourth time he was alarmed. The ghost child was standing in the workshop, near the doorway to the small kitchen, waving to him. He tried to speak to it, but it disappeared.

The most worrying thing for the whole family was the risk to their business. When the stone throwing was at its height John even spoke to his insurance company about the danger to customers. In fact, only one customer was hit, and not hard enough for injury to be caused, but she left the shop indignantly because she believed one of the staff had fired the missile at her. John and Pat were concerned that publicity would affect them adversely.

'I never believed in any of this before. I would have thought someone was nuts if they said all this had happened to them,' said John. 'So I thought people would think I was nuts.'

Two things rule out the possibility of faking in this case: the family's lack of motive for it and the substantial number of people who would have to be in on any plot. None of the people involved with the business stood to gain the slightest advantage from having Pete there and they all carefully avoided publicity. The incidents have happened over such a long period of time, and with such a variety of witnesses, that there can be no question of one person faking it all: the minimum number of people involved would have to be five or six, because events have occurred even when none of the four main family members was present. (Dr Fontana witnessed throwing while on his own in the workshop.)

Dr Fontana scrupulously investigated the possibility of underground water or vibrations from traffic or other physical events causing disturbance in the building. He went to the premises on numerous occasions, often unannounced, and never saw anything that made him suspect trickery. (Although Graham, John's original partner, was a practical joker and was known at times to flick stones about when everything was otherwise quiet. Graham's leaving the business did not end Pete's activity, and there were plenty of times before that when things occurred and Graham was not present.)

The case was ideal for investigation because the activity has lasted a long time and the poltergeist has not been shy about performing in front of strangers.

'The chances of getting another case as good as this are slim,' said Dr Fontana. 'It is the sheer volume of activity and the number of witnesses, many of whom I have tracked down and interviewed, that make it special. Poltergeists sometimes will not "perform" in front of anyone except the inhabitants of the house or building and investigators have to take a great deal on trust. That has been partly true with Pete. I have sometimes gone to the workshop when John has rung to say there was a lot of activity, only to find nothing happens while I am there. But I have also been able to witness actual phenomena and, on many occasions, I have seen the results of activity (for instance, the shop floor and counter covered in seed).

'It is very time consuming investigating a case like this, but very rewarding. The amount of activity was so great that at times I had to guard against getting blasé – I'd find myself feeling bored with the stone-throwing games and wishing something else would happen. Yet I know that most investigators would be delighted to witness and take part in reciprocal stone throwing with a poltergeist.

'I was also intrigued by my own reactions. When I was there, I would eliminate all possibilities of fraud or natural causes and would know that I was seeing genuine phenomena. But as soon as I was away from the premises and reflecting on what I had seen, I would find myself trying to reject the evidence of my own senses by coming up with all sorts of tortuous rationales for what was happening.'

The Cardiff case is still being monitored, and will probably become one of the Society for Psychical Research's celebrated cases. One of the most unusual features about it is that, unlike most poltergeist cases, it is not centred on an adolescent or young person, nor are any of the main participants emotionally unstable. John Matthews points out that the highest peak of Pete's activity coincided with his business going through a bad time: two very dry summers had reduced the need for lawnmowers, and consequent lawnmower repairs. But he and his relatives are equable people, old enough to have lived through other vagaries in their business life and uninclined to let problems get them down.

Another unusual feature is the reciprocal nature of the phenomena. At one time, it was possible to ask Pete to start throwing stones more or less at will. It was possible to ask not just for paper clips but for coloured paperclips and even to name the colour.

The word 'poltergeist' is German for noisy spirit (although the Germans themselves do not use the word, preferring 'spuk') and a noisy spirit is certainly present in the Cardiff case. Poltergeists and ghosts are generally regarded as different phenomena, although there are so many overlaps in the definitions of the two that it is not always possible to keep them apart. Classically, a ghost is an apparition which goes about its own business, regardless of whoever or whatever is around. Haunted houses, with their tales of headless knights, cowled monks and grey ladies, abound. The apparition can be seen, perhaps frequently, but it does not interact with those who see it.

A poltergeist, on the other hand, does interact. The Cardiff case is exceptional: most are not as intelligent or as responsive as Pete. But poltergeist cases always involve some attempt, however crude, to monopolize the attention of the living. Typical poltergeist activity includes rapping and making other noises, moving around ornaments and furniture, 'bringing' objects from other places. When small items are seen moving they often appear to travel as though being carried and, instead of losing height in a gradual trajectory, fall as though dropped. Although poltergeists rarely harm anyone, they can be destructive of property and they can pinch or push human beings. Some poltergeists produce water in unexplained pools, some seem to make objects hot to touch. There have been changes over the years. Before this century, cases did not involve switching on and off electric lights or causing electrical equipment to malfunction, and there are now more cases involving water, probably because today buildings are linked to the mains water supply. On the other hand there are fewer cases today of one of the poltergeists' nastier habits, the daubing of excrement, possibly because there are far fewer cess pits around.

These two groups, ghosts and poltergeists, are separated by large grey areas which overlap, or fit into neither category. The Cardiff case involved an apparition and, in other ways, it was outside the norm for poltergeist cases. The most common reported paranormal incidents do not fit into the definition of either ghosts or poltergeists and deserve a category of their own: hauntings. Like ghosts, these are centred on a place not a person, but they do not involve an apparition. Their standard trademarks are raps, imitative noises, voices, luminous effects and the opening and closing of doors.

Despite the limitations of this arbitrary breakdown, most investigators believe it is easier, if not always completely accurate, to categorize phenomena in one of these three groups: ghosts, hauntings or poltergeists.

There is no shortage of material to categorize, although the numbers of properly attested and witnessed cases are not as great as might be expected. Poltergeists have probably come in for the most investigative attention, simply because they make their presence so powerfully felt and are so disruptive that their hosts seek help. Hauntings are not so threatening and many old inns, hotels and stately homes regard ghosts as attractions. Plenty of families cheerfully co-exist with them.

Dr Alan Gauld, lecturer in psychology at Nottingham University, and his partner Tony Cornell have carried out the most exhaustive and credible study of poltergeists in the world. Gauld and Cornell teamed up many years ago, when Gauld was a student at Cambridge and Cornell was living and working in the town. They met through the Cambridge University Society for Psychical Research and, although their partnership is not a formal one and both have done many investigations independently, they still tend to work together much of the time. Gauld, a somewhat laconic intellectual, injects the academic contribution, and it is his work that makes up the statistical core of their book, *Poltergeists*. Cornell is a tireless enthusiast for field research, described by other members of the SPR as the action man of the pair. They share a sense of humour, a dedication to rooting out conscious or unconscious fraud and natural causes and a reluctance to commit themselves to explanations. In Gauld's case, this is probably the natural caution of the academic: he takes great pains to eliminate all other possible explanations except a paranormal one and then says that he does not necessarily accept that anything paranormal happened. Cornell's reluctance is more straightforward: he came to psychical research after an incident that convinced him that the paranormal existed, but his quest for it ever since has left him with only a small residue of evidence. He says that as he gets older (he's in his sixties), he is less and less sure what it is he is pursuing. None the less, his persistence and the evidence that he does have, belie his words.

The incident that awakened Tony Cornell's interest in the paranormal happened when he was in India with the army. He went to visit a fakir (a Hindu holy man), who had a considerable local reputation as a mystic. While talking to him, the fakir asked Cornell to turn away for a few seconds. When he turned round again, the fakir was on the other side of a wide river.

'It was a perfect case of levitation. But, over the years, I have tried to explain it away. At one time, I thought the fakir had hypnotized me and then suggested to me what I thought I saw, but I have since learned that I cannot be hypnotized – various experts have tried. I've also wondered whether I had sunstroke but, if I did, I recovered very quickly. Who knows?'

Cornell's experience came after a childhood with a mother who was 'sensitive' and who made various telepathic links with him and other members of the family. Although as a teenager he reacted against it, his experience in India made him interested enough to embark upon a lifetime's study of the paranormal.

Dr Alan Gauld's interest stretches back into his childhood and he too says he has inherited it from his mother. At Cambridge in the 1950s, he spent a night with other students involved in the University's Society for Psychical Research in a reputedly haunted house, with such marked results that he has been hooked ever since. He is critical of laboratory parapsychology, comparing it to a seismologist replicating tiny earthquakes in a lab while the buildings around shake as the result of real earthquakes. Not that he thinks evidence for the paranormal is often as dramatic or as quantifiable as an earthquake, but he believes that it must be studied out in the field where it happens spontaneously. He has encountered many puzzling and unexplained phenomena, but he is very slow to draw paranormal conclusions. In his own private life, too, he has been faced with the inexplicable. Twenty years ago, when his second son was newly born and his older son was three years old, he and his wife Sheila were watching a television programme about the birth of a baby.

'Sheila was fascinated, I was trying not to look. Just after the baby was born on screen we heard our older son crying upstairs. When Sheila went to him he said "Mummy, lady went into hospital, took off her clothes and had a baby." There was no possible way that he could have seen or heard anything from the television set, and the only explanation seems to be some telepathic link between him and his mother. We had another instance of it a few weeks later when Sheila, who is vegetarian, was upset witnessing rabbits being shot as they ran across a field in a television programme. Our son again seemed to have picked up the scene, because he said "Rabbits were running, running". Those were the only two occasions it happened and it seemed to have some connection with Sheila's heightened emotional state at each time. How can that be reproduced in a laboratory?'

Like Tony Cornell, Alan Gauld's experience in trying to isolate and define the paranormal outside the laboratory has not made him optimistic about easy solutions:

'I am less optimistic than I was about the prospect of readily coming to any answers. I have encountered a lot of fraud and natural causes and I've become a lot more cautious. I, and other psychic researchers, have incidentally become experts on all sorts of things like plumbing, building research, underground water but, ultimately, it is impossible to say that we have excluded everything.'

In their book, Gauld and Cornell offer powerful evidence for the existence of poltergeists and ghosts, even if they remain equivocal about their origins and causes. Dr Gauld has computer analysed five hundred cases, all of them well documented, although not necessarily contemporary (the oldest dates back to AD 530, seventy per cent occurred after 1800 and forty per cent during this century). Through complicated statistical analysis of sixty-three different possible characteristics for each case, he has effectively proved that there is a definable difference between hauntings and poltergeists, despite the overlap of characteristics between the groups, and that the basis of categorization is whether the phenomena are based on a person or a place.

Traditionally, poltergeists were centred on young adolescent girls but, in the later cases studied by Gauld, there has been a distinct upswing in the number of men acting as the central poltergeist 'agent'. Other research shows that the age profile of the agent has changed too, with more elderly people involved. (It has been suggested that the isolation of older people, and the consequent unhappiness it brings, may be making them more ready hosts for poltergeist phenomena.) Some sort of disturbance in the agent does seem to be a common factor and adolescence is often a time of acute emotional upheaval.

Why should poltergeist activity be triggered by some people and not others who are under equal stress? Can the agents in any conscious way control what happens around them? The answer to the second question would appear to be, only when there is a fraudulent element (and some young people, carried away with the attention they get when phenomena first start, cheat to keep their 'poltergeist' going). The answer to the first question must be that nobody knows: there has been no thorough comparison of the personality profiles of poltergeist agents.

Two of the most celebrated person-based poltergeist cases are the Rosenheim case (in Germany in 1967 and 1968) and the Miami case (in Florida, also in 1967). These two cases are now standard in poltergeist literature because they were investigated so well, the phenomena persisted long enough for good records to be made and kept and because the evidence appears to be irrefutable.

John Stiles, the investigations officer of the Society for Psychical Research and a noted sceptic who has never experienced anything paranormal in his life, says that the Rosenheim case is the only piece of evidence he has looked into that makes him believe that poltergeists exist.

The poltergeist activity occurred in the offices of a well-established lawyer's practice in the small German town of Rosenheim. Anne-Marie Schneider, aged eighteen, was a secretary in the Rosenheim office and fairly new to the job. Shortly after she joined, the entire office was reduced to chaos. Light bulbs would swing wildly and explode, showering glass everywhere; fluorescent ceiling lights would go out, sometimes with a bang. (On one occasion, electricians found that the fluorescent tubes throughout the building had been twisted ninety degrees in their sockets. After replacing them all, there was another bang and the same distortions were found in the new tubes.) Fuses blew with monotonous regularity; sometimes cartridge fuses seemed to have been pulled out of their sockets.

Problems with the telephones were the most severe inconvenience for the lawyer's business. Frequently, all four telephones would ring at once when no one was on the line. Calls were interrupted or cut off. Telephone bills rose astronomically and the office was charged for numerous calls that the staff denied making. Developing fluid from photocopying machines would spill while nobody was near the machine.

Because the disturbances appeared to be confined to electrical and telecommunications equipment, the lawyer called in the appropriate authorities. Experts from both the electricity supply company and the telephone company were able to install monitoring equipment which gives some factual non-human record of what went on. The local power station's monitoring showed up large irregular surges in the power supply and these continued even after, bewildered, they installed a generator to guarantee a continuous regulated supply of electricity to the offices.

The telephone company's findings were even more surprising. By recording every outward call, what time it was made and how long it lasted, they found that over a few weeks many calls were made to the speaking clock, often at the rate of six times in a minute, and at times when it is certain that nobody in the office could have been responsible. On one day, forty-six calls were made to the clock in a fifteen-minute period.

With so many staff and technicians in on what was happening, it is hardly surprising that news got out to the local press and, as a result, two television companies made short documentaries about the phenomena. The lawyer, at his wit's end because his office was being destroyed daily, and business and staff morale were suffering, filed a formal charge with the police against the (unknown) mischief maker. He hoped that, if he were the victim of an elaborate practical joke, this would persuade whoever was doing it to stop. The local CID launched an investigation.

By this stage, Professor Hans Bender, Professor of Parapsychology at the University of Freiburg, Germany, had arrived on the scene with some colleagues, including two physicists who took over the investigation of the electricity supply and the telecommunications equipment. They recorded erratic power deflections and loud bangs, and eliminated causes such as static magnetic fields, variations in the electric current, ultrasonic effects (including vibrations) and, amongst other things, manual intervention or faking.

Bender and his team soon decided that Anne-Marie Schneider was the focus of the activity, which always occurred during office hours, and sometimes started the moment she crossed the threshold. His announcement that he believed they were dealing with a poltergeist precipitated a greater variety of phenomena: paintings began to swing and even turn over on their hooks; decorative plates fell off the walls; drawers opened and closed by themselves; a heavy filing cabinet moved about a foot away from the wall. A video film was made of one of the pictures rotating.

As the investigation progressed, Anne-Marie became more and more nervous and hysterical. Eventually, she was sent home on leave and, immediately, all the problems stopped. She found another job and, although a few disturbances happened at her new place of work, there was nothing so dramatic and eventually these died away. The lawyer's office remained peaceful after she left. There were about forty witnesses who had observed the phenomena, including the technical experts, clients of the lawyer, journalists and scientists, as well as the staff at the office.

There are some marked similarities between this case and the occurrences in Miami during the same year. In both instances, the poltergeist activity occurred at the workplace of the agent. Personality-profile tests have shown that both agents have some characteristics, which might be important, in common. Both, for example, seemed to have felt some aggression towards those with whom they worked, but were able somehow to displace their aggression into poltergeist activity. (Both, incidentally, had forbearing and long-suffering employers. Other similar cases may be lost to research because employers would justifiably become fed up with such a catalogue of disturbance.)

In the case of the Miami poltergeist, the agent was a nineteen-year-old boy. Julio Vasquez, a Cuban refugee, was a clerk working in the warehouse of a wholesale company dealing in cheap souvenirs and novelty items. The warehouse contained tiers of shelves arranged in aisles and on the shelves were stacked and stored the goods to be supplied to retailers. Many of the items were breakable and many of them were broken, because Julio appeared to cause them to jump off the shelves and smash on the floor, even if he was at the other end of the warehouse.

The strange happenings at the warehouse came to the attention of a writer of popular books on parapsychology, Susy Smith. She was answering questions on a radio phone-in when a member of the warehouse staff called and told her, over the air, what was going on. Smith alerted two prominent American psychical researchers: W.G.Roll, Director of the Psychical Research Foundation in North Carolina, and Professor J.G. Pratt from the University of Virginia. Miss Smith and the two academics witnessed and recorded the astonishing effect Julio appeared to have on the goods on the shelves, detailing two hundred and twenty-four separate incidents in their reports. These were probably only the tip of the iceberg: the Julio effect had been felt for three or four weeks before they became involved and there were days when objects were falling from the shelves more or less non-stop.

The police had been called in more to pacify the other employees than because the owners of the warehouse held Julio to blame. The poltergeist was not shy: four police officers witnessed what was happening, as did several other independent witnesses apart from the staff and the parapsychologists. Among these witnesses was a professional magician, a friend of the owners, who had been unable to spot any possible fraud by Julio or anyone else.

Because the phenomena were fairly straightforward and confined to the area of the warehouse, it was relatively easy to arrange good scientific controls to monitor both Julio and his effect. From vantage points at opposite corners of the warehouse the two parapsychologists were able to make careful notes of who was where and when and Julio's position relative to anything falling off the shelves. The sheer amount of detailed information they were able to supply, though in many ways tedious and repetitive compared to some of the more exciting poltergeist activities in other cases, makes this one of the strongest cases ever recorded.

On one occasion, the object that fell off the shelf travelled twenty-two feet before it hit the ground. In other instances, a souvenir would leapfrog items in front of it on the shelves and crash to the floor. Sometimes the broken items had been deliberately placed on the shelves by the investigators in positions which seemed to particularly attract the poltergeist activity. Concerted efforts were made to discover natural or fraudulent causes for the succession of breakages: shelves were shaken and prodded, dry ice was used to balance objects precariously on the edge of shelves (with the result that they fell when the ice melted), but the researchers were left with no explanation of how objects from the back of shelves fell. Despite the close scrutiny under which he was held, nobody found any evidence of Julio faking the disturbances. He was a rather mixed-up and unhappy young man, pining for his mother and grandmother who had been left behind in Cuba and facing the prospect of having to move out of his stepmother's house. There was no doubt that he was under stress. After leaving his job at the warehouse, Julio served a short prison sentence for shoplifting and he was later shot while refusing to hand over the takings from the petrol station where he worked to two armed robbers. Since then, his life, according to Roll, has settled down and there have been no more paranormal phenomena.

One of England's most famous – and most controversial – poltergeist cases is the Enfield case, investigated by two members of the Society for Psychical Research, Maurice Grosse and Guy Lyon Playfair. The case lasted for eighteen months, starting in August 1977, and centred round one family: a divorced mother and her four children, thirteen-year-old Rose, eleven-year-old Janet, ten-year-old Pete and Jimmy, aged seven. It started with furniture moving about and rapping noises in the family's Enfield council house and progressed through some of the most startling phenomena reported: there were levitations, fires, water appeared from nowhere, excrement was daubed, apparitions were seen, writing appeared on walls and the two girls apparently developed the ability to talk with the voice of an old man, using language and vocabulary that were alien to them. Playfair wrote a book, *This House is Haunted*, giving a chronology of the case, which attracted media attention from all over the world. The book shows how the poltergeist, whose agent was originally thought to be Janet, could have moved around amongst different members of the family.

The case attracted controversy as vigorously as it attracted publicity. Other psychical researchers were not happy with the protocols established by Grosse and Playfair. There were suspicions that the children were colluding in fraud and that other witnesses were affected by the hysteria that was generated. At best, several of them feel that there may have been genuine poltergeist activity in the first few weeks at Enfield but that, from then on, the children enjoyed the attention they were getting and fabricated phenomena to keep up the interest. Ventriloquists and magicians were called in, as well as mediums and psychiatrists.

Maurice Grosse is hurt by any suggestions that the case was not genuine. He committed a great deal of his time and energy to investigating it and fifteen years later, with a number of other investigations under his belt, still feels that it was 'the case of the century'.

'It is very easy to cry "fakery" when we don't have any real answers,' he said. 'We have theories about poltergeists but we don't understand them. Fraud is one of the handiest explanations to latch on to. It stops us having to delve any further. I know the problem other researchers had – they didn't see what was happening at Enfield. It is one thing hearing about phenomena, quite another to witness them. It was my first investigation and I saw more startling evidence there than most researchers see in a lifetime of different cases.'

Maurice Grosse has tape recordings of various aspects of the case, including the gruff voice the girls could produce. Photographs were also taken, some of which purport to show the girls being thrown out of bed, their bedding whipped off them and levitations. Unfortunately, no video film was obtained of the phenomena. There was a persistent tendency for electrical equipment, mains or battery, to malfunction at the Enfield house.

Ghosts and Hauntings

When Andrew Green and his wife moved into a new house in Bramley, Surrey, the garden was what attracted them. It was an acre in size, and relatively undeveloped, with a wooded area and a trout stream running through it. A very keen gardener, Andrew spent most of his leisure time working on it. It preoccupied him – he even daydreamed about it while commuting into London to his publishing job. His favourite spot was a large rockery in one corner, which he built entirely alone, lugging heavy rocks into place and spending hours browsing through catalogues and garden centres to decide which plants to put in.

Unfortunately, Andrew and his wife divorced and had to move. They sold the house to a couple with two young children. During the sale, Andrew became friendly with the couple and invited them to call on him if ever they were passing through Robertsbridge in Sussex, where he now lives. Eighteen months later, they rang to say they would be in the area and would pop in to see him, bringing their children, who had never met Andrew, with them.

'As they got out of the car, their twelve-year-old daughter went very pale and fainted. When we got her up and into the house, she told her father that I was the man she had seen on the rockery. Apparently, she had been telling her parents for some time that she kept seeing a man on the rockery in the garden. They had not believed her, although her description had sounded quite like me. After meeting me in the flesh, she never saw me again in the garden.'

Andrew Green admits that it was an enormous wrench for him to leave the garden at Bramley and that he felt especially attached to the rockery because it was entirely his own work. At his new home, he woke up several times imagining he was back there.

'Obviously, the attachment wore off and I suspect that as it did the girl no longer saw me.'

Andrew Green appears to have been able to leave some sort of imprint of himself on the surroundings that were so important to him. It seems more likely that he created the apparition, than that it was created by the girl who had never clapped eyes on him before. Yet many experts say that all apparitions are hallucinations. They get round the problem of different people at different times seeing the same ghost by suggesting that the hallucination is transferred from one person to another by telepathy. In some way, the emotions of the first person to see the ghost transmit themselves to others at the scene and they then share the hallucination.

A classic group hallucination was reported by F.W.H. Myers in 1903 and happened in 1887. Canon Bourne and his two daughters went out hunting and at midday the two girls decided to return home with the coachman while their father carried on. After stopping to speak to somebody, they turned and saw the Canon waving his hat to them from the opposite side of a small dip and signalling to them to follow him. One of the sisters, Louisa Bourne, provided the following statement, which was also signed as correct by her sister:

'My sister, the coachman and I all recognized my father

and also the horse. The horse looked so dirty and shaken that the coachman remarked he thought there had been a nasty accident. As my father waved his hat I clearly saw the Lincoln and Bennet mark inside, although from the distance we were apart it ought to have been utterly impossible for me to have seen it. At the time I mentioned seeing the mark, though the strangeness of seeing it did not strike me until afterwards.

'Fearing an accident, we hurried down the hill. From the nature of the ground we had to lose sight of my father, but it took us very few seconds to reach the place where we had seen him. When we got there, there was no sign of him anywhere, nor could we see anyone in sight at all. We rode about for some time looking for him, but could not see or hear anything of him. We all reached home within a quarter of an hour of each other. My father then told us that he had never been in the field in which we saw him the whole of that day. He had never waved to us and had met with no accident. My father was riding the only white horse that was out that day.'

The fact that the girl could clearly see the manufacturer's mark in her father's hat at a distance from which it should not have been visible supports the hallucination theory, but there is still the problem of why all three of them saw exactly the same thing at the same moment, unless the apparition came not from their minds but from the mind of the Canon.

The hallucination theory may even hold good for the straightforward apparitions that manifest in the same place, doing the same thing, at different times (classic grey ladies and headless riders reported across the centuries). Fred, who saw the child-like apparition in the Cardiff poltergeist case, actually suggested to Dr Fontana that it might be his own hallucination of himself as a child.

Trying to make all cases conform to the theory is at best a tortuous exercise, and one that is rejected by researchers like Dr Alan Gauld who feels it falls short of explaining the physical phenomena that sometimes attend hauntings:

noises, the breaking of crockery, opening and closing doors with visible turning of handles or lifting of latches.

If the hallucination theory is accepted, it's interesting to note that the human mind can collectively conjure up the personality of a ghost.

Tony Cornell and some friends were called in to investigate a haunted pub, the Ferryboat Inn at Holywell, near Cambridge, in the early 1950s. Cornell had heard that every St. Patrick's Day a ghost appeared in the bar and pointed at one of the flagstones, which moved. He and his friends went there on the right day, stationed themselves above the flagstone with a ouija board, and conducted a seance. They soon had a communicator, a girl who told them her name was Juliet Tewsley, that she was a Norman, and that she was hanged for her affair with a married man, Thomas Zole, in 1054.

'There were five of us round the ouija board, possibly talking to our own unconscious minds. But it gave the landlord of the pub an idea, and he asked us to go again the following year – only for us to find that a lot of media people had also been invited. Since then, the story has been added to and added to,' said Tony Cornell.

'There is no evidence that this girl existed. The name Juliet didn't come into the English language until the sixteenth century, the Normans did not invade until 1066. One wonders if this is how all ghost stories start.'

In a more controlled way, the Toronto Society for Psychical Research created their own ghost in 1974. Eight of them, under the supervision of British mathematician Dr A.R.G. Owen, assembled around a table with their hands clearly visible on top and made 'contact' with a ghost they had invented themselves: a Royalist knight at the time of the English civil war, called Philip. Philip would answer questions by rapping on the table, and would make the table tilt and eventually levitate off the ground. But the framework of the fictional Philip's life had all been worked out beforehand by the group: he lived in a large house called Diddington Manor, he had a wife called Dorothea and had been passionately in love with a gypsy girl who was burned as a witch. Philip died by committing suicide, out of guilt for not having saved the girl. The 'ghost' of Philip accepted the characteristics assigned to him and even filled in more background details about himself.

Despite each member of the group suspecting the others of cheating, there was never any evidence of it, and some of the physical phenomena staggered everyone present. It was traditional for the group to hand around sweets, leaving one for Philip. On one occasion, when one of them jokingly tried to take Philip's sweet, the table tilted alarmingly away from him, but the sweet did not slide down it. Neither did others that were put next to it.

The group embarked on 'creating' Philip because they were interested in recording physical phenomena. They did not create an apparition of him, but the experiment demonstrates that the mind can create a ghost personality.

Hauntings have been reported since time immemorial. There are many references to them in classical literature. Because their manifestations are generally less dramatic and more sporadic than poltergeist cases, researchers have been present at fewer hauntings when phenomena have occurred, although there are well-attested cases of several witnesses experiencing the same phenomena. Most cases which are quoted in books on the supernatural as prime examples of hauntings are old. This is probably less to do with the frequency or quality of hauntings and more to do with the amount of time and interest available to record them properly. There are reputedly haunted houses in every district of Britain but remarkably few in which independent witness statements have been logged and compared.

The Despard case, which was first reported in 1892, is accepted as a classic and is still being studied and scrutinized in detail by researchers (it is often referred to as the Morton case, after the man who first wrote about it). A 'tall woman in black' was seen so often in the Despard family home in Cheltenham that some guests took her for another visitor. The woman always held a handkerchief to the lower part of her face. Unlike many apparitions, she was not confined to one spot but moved around the house and grounds. She was able to walk through objects and trip wires rigged deliberately to catch her. When a circle of people joined hands around her, she passed through the circle between two people and disappeared. Altogether, seventeen people bore witness to having seen her, some of whom had no prior knowledge of her 'presence' in the house. There were other assorted phenomena reported: footsteps, doors banging, handles turning.

According to Tony Cornell and Dr Alan Gauld, 'minor hauntings', where there are sounds, objects are moved and lights are switched on and off, but where there is no apparition, are far more common than poltergeists or ghosts. Yet because these cases are difficult to assess (and perhaps because they are rather dull) they do not find their way into case collections and parapsychological literature. Cases are also extremely hard to categorize, many of them overlapping the apparition and minor haunting groupings. One case Cornell and Gauld report in their book, *Poltergeists*, is the story of a haunting that took place in 1971 and 1972, in a substantial five-bedroomed detached house lived in by a married couple, who were both college lecturers, and their four children. After moving into the house, they experienced an assortment of phenomena: a spoon was seen suspended in mid air, a stone which had come out of a ring was moved from inside a jewel box to the bed, a noise was heard as if a trunk was being dragged across the landing, the sound of drawers being opened and closed was heard on numerous occasions, and one of the daughters and her cousin reported seeing an apparition during the night, a man who stood near the mantelpiece in the lounge with his head on his hands. Breathing noises, singing, a voice with a Scottish accent, footsteps and muffled whispers were all heard. The front door bell rang, and so did the telephone, when there was no one there. Gauld and Cornell believe the family were excellent witnesses, and say so in their book:

'When one investigates such cases on the spot, and meets the people concerned, the evidence even in the most superficially impressive examples tends to crumble before one's eyes; but sometimes the witnesses on better acquaintance seem so careful and so conscientious that one can neither dismiss nor yet completely explain away their cases. This was a case of the latter sort.'

One of Cornell's recent cases involved a newly-married couple who went on honeymoon to a fifteenth-century hotel in a market town in Norfolk.

'They knew nothing about the hotel, which was reputedly haunted, and they were a pragmatic pair who resolutely did not believe in ghosts. Although they were just married, they had been living together for some years. They had been given the three-night honeymoon as a surprise present from the bride's father, and had only been told about it that day. They had no chance to learn anything about the history of the hotel,' he said.

The couple arrived in the evening, had dinner, and went up to their room at about nine o'clock. The door at first refused to open and they both noticed that there was a cold spot outside it. Once inside the room they felt it was cold, despite the fact that the radiators were working normally. It was a typical honeymoon room, with a four poster bed on one side and an open fireplace on the other. Above the fireplace was a piece of glass, covering and protecting an old fresco. As they settled down in bed they both noticed a luminous glow coming from one side of the fireplace. They were puzzled but not disturbed and settled down for the night.

At about half past eleven, they heard someone pacing up and down in the corridor outside their room, then they heard the footsteps inside the room. They both got out of bed to investigate but could see nothing, although they could hear the footsteps going round the foot of the bed. Between three and four o'clock in the morning the husband woke up and saw a young girl, aged between about twelve and fifteen, with a garland of flowers in her hair. As he nudged his wife to waken her, the figure walked to the window and disappeared.

The following day, when they mentioned their experiences to the manager of the hotel, he told them that the American guest in the room next to theirs had also had a disturbed night and had checked out of the hotel. The manager offered them a different room, but despite having by this time heard the history of the haunting, they decided they would stay where they were. The story they were told was that three hundred years previously the owner of the inn, a woman, had been having an affair with an ostler who murdered her in that room. Her daughter, who had been having an affair with the same man, threw herself off the balcony when she learned of her mother's death.

On the second night, they again had problems opening the door of the room, but this time the room was so hot they had to open a window. Once again, there was a luminous glow by the fireplace and again they heard footsteps both inside and outside their room. During the night the husband felt the bedclothes being pulled over his head. This happened three times.

In the morning, the manager showed them a portrait of the owner who legend said had been murdered. The husband was shocked because he recognized her as an older version of the girl he had seen. That night they experienced the same problems opening the door to their room and saw the glowing light. On closely inspecting the room they found a hand print, the size of a child's hand, on the inside of the glass covering the wallpainting. The glass, which was held about an inch and a half proud of the wall by a heavy wooden frame, was quite dusty on the inside and the fresh print showed up clearly.

In the early hours of the morning, the husband again woke up and saw the same girl sitting on the end of the bed. He believed he could actually feel the depression caused by her weight. For about fifteen seconds she and he looked at each other and then she once again went to the window and disappeared. When she left, he felt the springs of the bed go up. In the morning another set of fingerprints could be seen on the glass.

When he investigated the haunting, Tony Cornell was

satisfied that the couple were truthful and sincere, and as they had both been firm disbelievers in anything paranormal, there appeared to be no obvious motivation for fraud. But his investigations showed that the owner of the hotel whose picture was hanging in the lounge had died a natural death, had not had a daughter and that there was no record of her having an affair with an ostler.

'One of the problems with psychical research is that a lot of time is spent on cases that are eighty years old or more,' he said. 'But there are still some very good examples happening right now.'

Investigations

It seems odd that we have so little evidence of ghosts and poltergeists and hauntings, apart from witness testimony. Psychical researchers often report back that their cameras failed, their tapes broke, their film turned out to be blank. There is a very high rate of instrument failure on a field investigation.

With the high-tech equipment now available, instrument recording would seem to be the logical way forward. Infra-red cameras can record in the dark, without upsetting any 'atmosphere' necessary for whatever is going on, video equipment is becoming more compact, image intensifiers and all sorts of other sophisticated gear are available. Many members of the Society for Psychical Research agree that instrumentation is necessary. Unfortunately what is available has been assembled on an ad hoc basis, mostly at individual expense.

The best device in Britain at the moment is nicknamed SPIDER (Spontaneous Psycho-physical Incident Data Electronic Recorder), which has been devised and assembled by Tony Cornell, Alan Gauld and Howard Wilkinson, who is in charge of technical services in the psychology department at Nottingham University and who works with Cornell and Gauld on many of their field investigations. According to Wilkinson, SPIDER is a 'glorified burglar alarm'. It consists of a small Sinclair computer in a radiation-proof box, a printer with a series of relays which control infra-red, ultra-sonic and electro-static detectors, as well as video cameras, stills cameras, sound microphones and lights. A grant from the SPR paid for a time-lapse video recorder, but Cornell alone has invested about six thousand pounds in the equipment. He pioneered the assembly of the equipment with the help of two electronics students from Cambridge but, ultimately, it was Howard Wilkinson who assembled it, re-wired it and got it working.

The main drawback of SPIDER is its size: putting it in place involves trailing wires and inconveniently bulky hardware. It is, as Tony Cornell says: 'Absolutely no use in the average family home, especially if there are dogs, cats and children about. And if you need to cover more than one room at a time with the cameras, it becomes even more difficult.'

But Wilkinson, Cornell and Gauld are keen to use it wherever they can, so that ultimately they can assemble a library of video footage, not just as proof of the phenomena but also as a means of training other field investigators. They have made a start: they have one piece of video tape recording a poltergeist outbreak at a car-hire firm in Arnold, near Nottingham. The case began in August 1990 when an eighteen-year-old youth joined the firm to do the steam cleaning and valeting of their fleet of cars. Small gravel stones were being thrown at great velocity, narrowly but consistently missing people, around the portakabin premises the company was using. Observers were able to throw stones and see them come whizzing back. Milk bottles were rearranged and files floated off desks and dropped on to the floor.

Although in some instances the youth seemed to be cheating by flicking the stones himself, there were others when it was impossible for him to be responsible.

'On one occasion I was in the office with the lad and Alan was outside able to see everything,' said Tony Cornell. 'A stone hit the wall above his shoulder and dropped into a teacup. It was impossible for him to have faked it. And there were occasions when stones could be heard raining down on the roof while he was inside the portakabin. Sometimes as many as forty or fifty stones would be swept off the roof at the end of the day, and the local police had ruled out the possibility of vandalism.'

SPIDER was installed and a video was recorded of the steam arm coming off a steam-cleaning device.

'It was taken on a dim day at the back of the premises. The handle moved as someone walked past. It doesn't look as though he touched or nudged it. A clear noise is recorded. But, as luck would have it, the time and date on the tape recording partially obscures what happened,' said Howard Wilkinson. 'It is possible today to get edge detection equipment which analyses video tape frame by frame on a computer, blocking out anything which is stationary and only showing up movement.

'We need this equipment. We also need sound-analysis equipment. And we need to miniaturize what we already have, so that we don't have to hump a great load of gear about with us.'

Where possible, SPIDER is rigged up with two cameras per room, each in the field of view of the other to eliminate the possibility of tampering. Even after taking as many precautions as possible to ensure that his equipment is as tamper-proof as possible by using tape to secure cables and leads, however, Wilkinson has experienced an unusual number of 'technical' faults.

'I was very excited when I thought that at Arnold there would be some film recording chairs moving. I screeched down there to pick it up, but when I got the film back there was nothing on it. I checked all the equipment and it appeared to be in full working order, but eventually I realized that the F-stop on the camera had been changed so that it did not record in the dark. Everyone swore they had not touched it, and because I had by that time spent weeks on the case and knew them well, I was inclined to believe them, after initially feeling I'd been set up. On other occasions and other cases, I've had plugs pulled out of the back of recorders, even though they were taped in. Part of the psychology of dealing with these cases is deciding whether you believe that the people involved did it or not. We will always have the problem of making equipment tamper-proof: until we work out how "spirits" tamper with things!'

SPIDER has been tried out at the scene of various hauntings, without much success. It was installed for fifty-two days at Carnfield Hall, near Nottingham, a large home with a long history of haunting but the most that was recorded were a few strange photographs.

'One of the problems with hauntings is that they are so unpredictable,' said Tony Cornell. 'We're seriously thinking of advertising for anyone with a large stately home that is haunted to let us install the equipment in a part of the building where it would not be in anyone's way and where the haunting is supposed to happen.

'Failing to pick something up on the cameras does not necessarily mean that nothing happened. If someone clearly sees a ghost and it does not appear on the film, that tells us something about the nature of the phenomenon. We have to appraise every bit of technical evidence we get rigorously: so many doubtful photographs have been produced over the years, purporting to show paranormal events, and there seems to have been no effort to eliminate lens flares, double exposures, reflections of light off furniture . . .

'If we can get a lot more on video we will really have made a breakthrough. The advantage of filming something is that you can look back at it afterwards. Witnessing an event takes only a couple of seconds and, in retrospect, you start to query your own senses. Did I really see what I thought I saw? A film of it means you can look at leisure, picking up lots of things you missed at the time.'

Robin Furman runs an organization he calls Ghostbusters UK (it used to be called Grimsby Ghostbusters but they have spread their wings to take in the whole country). A psychotherapist who works from home, Furman and his son Andy, with Rodney Mitchell, a computer consultant, and Janice Paterson make up the Ghostbuster team, and, in great contrast to the low-key style of Dr David Fontana, Dr

Alan Gauld, Tony Cornell and other serious investigators, they court publicity. They travel to their cases in a 1959 Austin Princess, an ex-mayoral limousine, which they have dubbed the Ghostmobile. Furman says they do not have the registration plate ECTO 1 (as in the film *Ghostbusters*) but you get the impression that they would if they could.

The equipment the Ghostbusters use also has a cute name: they call it the Roboghost. It is an Acorn computer which can monitor changes in temperature, light and vibrations, as well as being attached to sound-recording equipment. Any change registers a blip on the screen of the computer and Furman and his crew are hoping to build up a sufficient body of printouts of different types of paranormal events to be able to find patterns.

At one house in Heston, Middlesex, the home of childminder Mrs Bessie Smith and her daughter Sharon, the Roboghost blipped as soon as it was plugged in. Sharon said she saw an ashtray whizz across a table. Unfortunately the CBS camera crew Furman had with him had not set up their filming equipment when the ashtray moved, and there were no more paranormal events that day. All in all, Furman said he identified twenty-one different types of incident in the Smiths' home, ranging from doors slamming and the sound of footsteps, to ornaments and milk-bottle tops being 'carried' through the air in full view of the family.

The Ghostbusters live on hype and so far have yet to produce any serious evidence or research. Robin Furman sees himself as providing a service more than as an academic researching the field.

'As it said in the film, who do you call when you've got a ghost? People don't know where to turn for help. Often the church no longer wants to know, and their neighbours and friends may treat them as though they have gone a bit nutty. We turn up, take them seriously, talk the whole thing through, and just by that alone we have helped solve the problem. Very often one visit by us and the Roboghost is enough to quieten everything down.

Sometimes an explanation is all it needs: if they know the ghost won't harm them they can get on with living with it. We do a bit of local research to find out who is doing the haunting and why. It puts their minds at rest, and often seems to be enough to persuade the ghost to leave them alone.'

Furman and his cohorts have actually performed exorcisms 'when I know it will help and when the people in the house expect it'. He believes he has mentally grappled with 'thought-forms' that were 'possessing' victims, and that he has managed to expel them.

Furman's methods might be considered eccentric by members of the SPR (although he is a member). The Society does not proselytize any particular views or beliefs, but tries to live up to the aim of its founding fathers: 'to approach these varied problems without prejudice or prepossession of any kind, and in the same spirit of exact and unimpassioned inquiry which has enabled Science to solve so many problems . . . '

Every year the Society is asked to investigate about fifty different cases, a disproportionate number in London and the Home Counties. Twenty per cent fizzle out before anyone can look into them, and the rest are farmed out to members of the Society who have expressed a willingness to investigate. John Stiles, who is responsible for dishing out the cases, generally allocates them on a geographical basis, although sometimes he will tell a particular investigator if he knows they have an interest in certain types of cases. There is a shortage of people willing to do investigations and the SPR are concerned that there is no way of training newcomers apart from sending them out with seasoned investigators.

One of the concerns of many of the best researchers in the field is to establish some protocols for classifying information on cases, so that they can be grouped and compared in much the same way that Dr Gauld analysed his five hundred cases, but with more emphasis on modern cases and with more ease because certain standard information will have been recorded each time. Professor Robert

Morris, who has the Koestler chair in Parapsychology at Edinburgh University, believes that research is sidetracked by the constant quest for proof.

'What happens when we have proof? Is the job done? If we are here to explain what is happening, that is just when the job begins, when the fun starts. When we get away from only seeking to prove, then our strategies and styles for collecting data are enlarged. We need a lot of information we don't always get from case investigators so that we can look for pattern, meaning and content. We must not forget the individual nature of each case, but we should pay more attention to integrating and comparing them.'

The majority of cases founder very quickly: they turn out to have natural causes, or it is immediately obvious that the people concerned are faking the phenomena (sometimes, as Professor Archie Roy, Professor of Astronomy at Glasgow University and founder of the Scottish Society for Psychical Research, points out because the family involved want to get a transfer to a different council house).

'We spend far more time on cases where there is nothing paranormal involved than we do on the gold nuggets of the real cases,' said Professor Roy.

In only eight per cent of the cases studied by Alan Gauld was fraud detected – but this figure takes no account of those in which the fraud went undetected, or those which were never written up in the records because fraud was uncovered quickly and immediately. He points out the danger, though, of falling into the trap of believing that because fraud was possible, it was necessarily what was happening. Feats that could be achieved by complex equipment or by accomplished magicians are beyond the reach of ordinary people and, unless there is any evidence to support the idea that they may be practised conjurors or mechanical geniuses, it is fair to assume they are not cheating.

'We have heard of only one case (and that at second hand) in which a poltergeist agent is said to have shown an interest in conjuring prior to the outbreak; and we know of no case in which a poltergeist agent has afterwards gone on to establish himself as a skilled stage conjuror,' Gauld and Cornell say in their book.

Trickery does seem to have been a component in quite a number of cases, though: as if the poltergeist sometimes needs a little bit of gentle prodding (as in the Cardiff case) to get it active. But trickery alone could account for only a tiny proportion of the phenomena.

Natural causes account for a substantial number of cases. One case of curious noises investigated by Gauld and Cornell turned out to be rats in the attic dropping apples that were stored there down through the cavity walls. Creaks and groans in central-heating pipes, water hammer, draughts that open and close doors – even an escaped convict who was hiding in a 'haunted' house and switching the lights on and off from time to time – have been weeded out by investigators.

One natural cause that proved not to be a cause was the underground-water theory. In the 1950s and 1960s, G.W. Lambert, a member of the SPR, formulated his theories that underground water channels (old sewers, subterranean streams and so on) caused movement of buildings, which in turn gave rise to 'supernatural' phenomena such as objects moving about and doors opening and closing. He and others also postulated that earthquakes, which were too small to register on instruments at seismic observatories, could be responsible.

To test the theory, Tony Cornell managed to negotiate from the Cambridge Borough Surveyor the right to try out some experiments on several houses which were due for demolition but which were sound and free of damp. With the help of Alan Gauld and others he staged an experiment in which one of the houses was subjected to strong vibrations and hit repeatedly with a sixty-pound weight. Various small objects had been placed around the house, on window ledges and fireplaces. Despite the fact that the vibrations were strong enough to be clearly felt in houses two or three doors away, nothing moved. When the weight was used, the exterior of the house was damaged and plaster fell off inside. Eventually, a camera tripod fell over, but nothing else moved. The series of experiments proved that any 'natural' vibrations or impacts would have to be enormously strong to cause ornaments and other objects to move about, as they routinely do in poltergeist cases.

The reliability of witnesses is another serious consideration for researchers. Work is going on at Edinburgh University to establish how well we see and report incidents that happen before our eyes. Professional conjurors make a living out of our inability to properly take in what happens in front of us, but research shows that, although we may miss important clues with our eyes, we do not use our imaginations to embroider the story afterwards. The saying 'the story grows in the telling' is wrong: as time goes by the reported event is not enlarged and may, in many cases, be diminished in the telling. When separate sets of accounts of the same incident are given by a witness with a gap of years between them, there is no exaggeration.

So what causes these events? When fraud and natural causes have been exhaustively investigated and rejected, what are we left with? We know that many poltergeists seem to be projections of the unhappy personality of the poltergeist agent; we know that many parapsychologists believe that ghosts and apparitions are all hallucinations created by our own minds. But these two explanations don't come close to covering the different kinds of phenomena produced in the wide range of individual cases studied. Despite several ingenious attempts to explain how the poltergeist agent makes things happen around him or herself, we are no nearer to understanding it.

The most interesting question is: whose intelligence is the poltergeist tapping into, or does it have its own? Pete the Poltergeist would not only throw stones back but could find tools from the workshop, produce paperclips of the colour specified and even, when asked for something useful, put his hand in his metaphorical pocket and bring out some used fivers.

Experts divide into those who believe everything comes from the mind of a living agent and others, like Dr Ian Stevenson of the University of Virginia, who believe that some are evidence of a force coming from outside a living human being, perhaps the spirit of someone who has died. Dr Gauld and Tony Cornell fit into this latter group. They accept that many cases are caused by living agents, but feel there are also a few cases which show intelligence of matters that could not be known to any living person present, not even by using ESP. They do not commit themselves on what type of entity may be providing the intelligence.

So there are no easy answers. And there are unlikely to be for many years, as the researchers point out. Many more detailed case studies are needed.

'It won't be explained in my lifetime,' said Tony Cornell. 'But it is just possible that my grandchildren will live to find out the cause.'

3
Examining the Evidence

When Bob Morris was a fourteen-year-old schoolboy his eyesight started to fail. So, when he finished his psychology degree some years later, he decided to specialize in parapsychology, because he thought that since it was a relatively new subject there would not be too much reading to strain his eyes. Luckily, it was only one of the reasons for his choice – and a minor one – because he has faced a prodigious amount of reading ever since. Parapsychology may be a Cinderella science, but it is a fruitful one, generating massive amounts of research material each year, as well as large numbers of books on allied subjects. Professor Morris, an American from Pittsburgh, is the most senior parapsychologist working in Britain, occupying the country's only chair in parapsychology at Edinburgh University. The chair was set up with half a million pounds left for the purpose in the joint will of the respected writer Arthur Koestler and his wife Cynthia, whose double suicide in 1982 shocked the literary world. Koestler was suffering from a debilitating disease and was in pain: Cynthia chose to die with him. They were both convinced of an afterlife and determined to reach it together, having been in the forefront of the campaign for voluntary euthanasia. They left the bulk of their estate to set up a British chair in parapsychology because both had been intensely interested in the subject. Koestler had written several books about it (one, *The Roots of Coincidence*, a seminal work that has inspired many young men and women to become involved in serious research work).

One of the executors of the Koestlers' estate was Dr John Beloff, a psychologist at Edinburgh University and a man with an abiding interest in the paranormal. Beloff was one of the few academics in Britain willing to accept and monitor the work of PhD students tackling aspects of parapsychology. As the only executor with any knowledge of the field, it fell primarily to him to find a British university at which to set up the chair. Cambridge, which would have been Koestler's first choice, was not interested and Oxford was only prepared to get involved if they could use the money to fund other research. The Prince of Wales supported the idea that the chair should go to Cardiff but, eventually, because of greater all-round support, Edinburgh University was chosen.

It is a measure of parapsychology's poor reputation within the academic world that the British universities, generally enthusiastic about large dollops of cash, were not fighting to get their hands on this endowment.

In 1985 Professor Morris was appointed. Bob Morris's interest in the paranormal was fostered almost from birth because both his parents were fascinated by it. A friend of the family had made an ESP testing device for them, an ingenious box which drops coloured marbles one at a time, allowing the experimenters to guess or influence the colour that appears next. As a young boy he tried the game out on friends and family and his interest in the subject deepened when he felt he was getting positive results.

'I liked the idea that the effect could be measured in a tangible way. Even then, as a child, I was less concerned with startling results than with the opportunity to measure results objectively.' He keeps the marble box in his office. 'Of course, we would never accept equipment like that in our lab testing, it is very unsophisticated. But it was responsible for triggering my interest and I'm fond of it.' When he went to university he admits he was naive enough not to know the distinction between psychology and psychiatry but, during his degree course in psychology, he became more and more fascinated by the work being done in parapsychology.

'I hung around the people working in the parapsychology department and got the impression that they were not all crazy. During my summer holidays as a postgraduate student, I started researching the subject and eventually went into it full time.'

Professor Morris's department at Edinburgh University has funding for three other parapsychologists – one permanent and one temporary post-doctorate fellow and one full-time research associate – and a secretary and has between four and eight postgraduate students attached to it at any one time. So what are they studying?

There are plenty of people, even among the informed members of the Society for Psychical Research, who seem to believe that after six or seven years of full-time work, the Edinburgh team should have demonstrated for good and all the existence of psi. The amateurs who give up so much of their own time – and would relish the prospect of being funded to work on it full time – cannot accept that progress in laboratory research is a painstakingly slow affair. They, like so many of the general public, thought that the Koestler money would buy instant results.

If instant results could be bought, the Americans would have had them years ago. If psi could be bottled and packaged in a lab, it would be on sale at a knockdown mail-order price in the USA, where over the last forty years big money has been invested in research.

One of the main problems with laboratory research is that paranormal phenomena are unpredictable. Ghosts and poltergeists cannot be taken into a laboratory to be clinically dissected and analysed, any more than crisis visions, out of body experiences and even plain old telepathy can be relied on to happen to order. And as for near-death experiences . . . The very nature of the subject makes it hard to study.

Since emotional stress and anxiety play a large part in stimulating some of the phenomena, it is virtually impossible (and, at any rate, unethical) to reproduce the stresses in controlled conditions in a laboratory. Although a few psychics – the so-called 'psi stars' – seem to be able to function under close scrutiny in unsympathetic surroundings, most are only able to perform in cosier, homelier situations.

Boredom is another factor working against the researchers. Predicting the colours of cards or marbles – or taking part in any of the thousands of other laboratory experiments that the parapsychologists have dreamed up to measure telepathy or psychokinesis in the lab – is a repetitive and mind-numbing exercise not inclined to spark unusual and intuitive reactions. In fact, research shows that the longer someone does the experiment, the poorer their psi performance is. Yet it is important to carry out long runs to produce any kind of meaningful statistic.

Parapsychology can never be an exact science. It cannot be compared to chemistry, where the same results can be obtained over and over again when the same chemicals are mixed together. It involves human beings and the unpredictable and immeasurable dimensions that this adds makes it a difficult subject for laboratory study. However, the parapsychologists are convinced that their subject will be given the respectability that they crave only when they have a single, repeatable laboratory experiment that can be carried out under the scrutiny of the most dedicated sceptics and produce the same result under whatever circumstances.

They have set themselves a tall order. Nobody working in, say, psychology or sociology (also inexact sciences that involve human variables) would expect to have one set-piece experiment that works in the same way under all conditions and with all people.

Although the parapsychologists have not managed to set up one neatly-packaged test that can provide proof to a sceptical public, they have come a long way and learned a lot about the nature of psi. Because progress is slow and the research brings no obvious pay-offs (although there are some, see chapter 8), funding across the world is not as easily available as it once was. By the time researchers moved into the laboratory, the paranormal was no longer a fashionable area.

There are always academics so fascinated by the subject that they are prepared to sink their careers into it; while others have the interest but are not prepared to spend their lives working in a discipline that is regarded as 'fringe' and not quite respectable and which offers few opportunities for advancement. When Dr John Beloff was one of the very few academics in Britain accepting PhD students in parapsychology, he wrote to every applicant telling them to consider seriously the career problems ahead. However, there are some rewards for those working in the field: because it is still a relatively new and unexplored subject, there is a great deal to do; and because nobody can prescribe what should be done and how the results should look, there is a great deal of freedom for the researcher. As Professor Morris discovered at the expense of his eyesight, the amount of reading material being generated at least equals and perhaps surpasses that created by more established and heavily-subscribed disciplines in which academics have to search diligently for tiny unexplored areas in which to make their name.

Every year the parapsychologists hold an annual convention, an academic get-together in which the best examples of new research are presented to their peers. The paperwork generated at just one convention weighs about three pounds and covers subjects as diverse and esoteric as 'Hemispheric assymetry, preconscious processing and paranormal processes' and 'Meta-analysis of DMT-ESP studies and an experimental investigation of perceptual defence/vigilance and extrasensory perception', as well as the jollier sounding 'Marijuana, psi and mystical experiences' and 'Poltergeist reports: a study of thirteen Brazilian cases'.

What exactly is parapsychology?

'The scientific study of paranormal phenomena, in particular the capacity attributed to some individuals to interact with their environment by means other than recognized sensory and motor channels' was the wording used when setting up the Koestler Chair in Edinburgh.

Professor Morris describes it as a challenge. 'My challenge was to develop and implement a sensible plan of attack on a problem area of considerable complexity, to allow a realistic but fair evaluation of a wide range of claims for special mental powers ... Such powers can be faked in ingenious ways, often very hard to detect. Also, we can easily be misled accidentally, in all innocence: the ways we acquire and interpret information about events around us are notoriously fallible.'

He says that he is eighty-five per cent sure that psi exists but sees his role as much as the devil's advocate as a proselyte (an interpretation that some of the diehard members of the SPR find hard to swallow: they believe there are enough sceptics attempting to demolish the case for psi without those who are supposed to be on the same side joining in). But Bob Morris is convinced that it is important to eliminate all possible means of deception, fake, fraud, trickery (deliberate or innocent) at source, so that the critics can be answered. That's why he was delighted to find a research student who was also a professional magician and a member of the Magic Circle. It has given him the opportunity to examine not just the ways in which fraud could be committed, but how even the most dedicated observers can be deceived and can misinterpret what they have seen (see chapter 7).

His critics believe he and his team should spend more time out in the field, getting to grips with the exciting side, the poltergeists and haunted houses. The difficulty of this is obvious: a full-time working life cannot be structured around things that may or may not go bump in the night.

So at Edinburgh, as in most serious research establishments in the world, the study of psi comes down to four areas:

TELEPATHY: the ability of two minds to communicate, to share thoughts and experiences without speech or any other direct link.

CLAIRVOYANCE: the ability to know about things beyond the natural range of the senses. (Technically speaking, this has to be information acquired by 'seeing' the event, not hearing about it,'clairaudience', or sensing it, 'clairsentience', but for most common purposes they are lumped together under clairvoyance, which colloquially means the acquisition of the knowledge by paranormal means, whatever the technique.) The distinctions between clairvoyance and telepathy are fine and it can be difficult to know whether information has been acquired telepathically or clairvoyantly.

PRECOGNITION: the ability to foresee events. (This is perhaps even more baffling than telepathy or clairvoyance, as it suggests that time may not be the straight arrow that we perceive it to be.) Retrocognition, or the ability to see into the past, is assumed to be another variant of the same phenomenon.

These three subjects can all be covered by the overall umbrella title of ESP, extra sensory perception, which simply means acquiring information by other than the normal means of our five senses, touch, taste, sight, hearing and smell.

The fourth basic area is PSYCHOKINESIS: the ability to move or influence the movement of physical objects without touching them – or, as it is commonly called, mind over matter. This embraces legendary miracles, laboratory experiments in which psi stars seem to be able to move objects, a great deal of poltergeist activity and even the ability of sports stars to 'psych themselves up' to greater achievements.

Again, there are sometimes difficulties deciding which of these four areas phenomena fit into. If someone can consistently predict the colour of playing cards, or the numbers on dice before they are thrown, or the numbers thrown up by a random-number generator (one of the parapsychologists' favourite bits of equipment), they could be using either precognition to foresee the numbers or psychokinesis to influence the numbers to be the ones they have chosen. None the less, as broad categories these four work well and exploration of them has spawned many varied tests.

There are not yet any staggering conclusions, although a

lot of the work demonstrates the possible existence of psi. 'A weak and noisy but nevertheless real effect, one deserving much closer scrutiny,' as Professor Morris puts it.

One of the main problems for the non-scientist is that the experts are always, necessarily, measuring their results against chance. This means their results become statistically significant long before they seem very impressive to the casual bystander.

For example, if we use five different playing cards and ask someone to predict which one is being laid on the table two hundred and fifty times, he should, by chance, get fifty calls right (one in five). But nobody would be surprised if he actually got forty-five or fifty-five: that is so close to the 'chance' score that we would not see it as statistically significant. The ordinary observer might expect a good demonstration of psi to come up with something like two hundred right (four hits out of every five calls). But to be statistically significant one only needs to get more than sixty-one right. According to the laws of chance, our guesser would only have a one in twenty chance of getting that many right and anything more than one in twenty is regarded by statisticians as significant. Psi researchers, though, knowing the scepticism of the public, like much better scores before they start getting excited. If the guesser got seventy of his two hundred and fifty calls right, that would be a one in one thousand hit rate, and they would see that as evidence that something other than chance was operating.

The rest of us, however, bred on television magic shows where there is no margin for wrong 'guesses', would not be sitting on the edge of our seats with excitment because somebody predicted seventy out of two hundred and fifty cards correctly.

So laboratory research into psi is hampered by the fact that it is dealing with figures which, although statistically and mathematically valid, do not impress Joe Public. Nor do they impress a lot of psychic researchers, those who feel that what goes on in the lab has very little to do with the rich world of spontaneous paranormal happenings.

Professor Archie Roy, Professor of Astronomy at Glasgow University and founder of the Scottish Society for Psychical Research, is not a critic of laboratory research because, as a scientist himself, he knows the importance of confounding critics with measurable and repeatable experiments. But even he describes the lab work in parapsychology as 'catching minnows in the fine net of statistics'.

Parapsychologists are aware of the problems confronting them. In recent years, they have worked at getting away from sterile conditions, making sure that people tested in labs are relaxed and in comfortable, homely surroundings.

'We know that putting emotion back in has to be done very very sensitively,' said Professor Morris. 'We have thought about using good method actors, who could really throw themselves into a role, but so far have not devised any experiments. We know that telling people to come into the laboratory between three and four on Tuesday afternoon and be psychic is pretty hopeless and could be causing weakened results. We hope that by setting up computer terminals in people's own homes, they will be able to choose when they want to do experiments, when they feel like doing them.

'We can set up a target in a sealed room and ask them to try to respond to it. We can give them a target to dream about and, then, when their dreams are recorded they can be "blind" judged by an independent person who will try to match them to the target. There are many possibilities for getting people to be tested in their own, friendly environment.'

Within the confines of a laboratory setting, parapsychologists have tried to create the best possible psychological state for psi, and to work out why some people are more likely to experience it than others. By working in these directions, they have come up with something that gets very close to that single repeatable experiment that they crave.

Ask any distinguished parapsychologist which of the hundreds of different experiments carried out over the last fifty or so years have produced the most impressive results and they will all include on their list the 'ganzfeld' work.

Ganzfeld is a German word meaning 'whole field' and the idea is to blur all the senses into one indistinct whole by cutting out all distractions and disturbances. It is a technique for putting human guinea pigs into the right mental state for their psi abilities to work, despite the fact that they are being monitored in a laboratory. Charles Honorton, the American parapsychologist who pioneered ganzfeld research, knew that in normal life people are most likely to experience ESP when they are in a relaxed state and when their minds are 'switched off'. In other words, when they are not concentrating on anything in particular, but are allowing their thoughts to range freely. This is why so many 'psychic experiences' occur in the twilight zone between sleep and wakefulness, when we are not controlling the direction of our minds as we have to during normal waking activities (why, too, drugs, alcohol, hypnosis and stress can all induce mystical or psychic experiences).

Honorton devised a way to get his subjects as close to this condition, known as an 'altered state of consciousness', as possible in an ethical, controlled way. He found that relaxing on a bed or a chair in comfortable surroundings helped. He covered his subjects' eyes with halved table tennis balls, sealed around the edges. The translucent material the balls are made of allows some light to filter through and experiments showed that red light is most relaxing, giving a warm pink glow through the eye-covers. Headphones block out all extraneous noise and the subjects are given a pleasant, rhythmic sound – like the lapping of waves on a beach – to listen to. An alternative is 'white noise', a nondescript background buzz. In a recent series of experiments at the Psychophysical Research Laboratories in Princeton, New Jersey, subjects were also given some teaching in the art of relaxation. Once comfortably settled, a 'sender' in another room attempted to relay a telepathic message to the 'receiver', the person in the ganzfeld. Research has shown that the best kind of messages to transmit are pictures and the best kind of pictures are moving ones. Generally, the sender is given a short video clip chosen at random to watch and asked to transmit it telepathically to the receiver.

As he lies there, relaxed and comfortable, the receiver talks out loud, describing the pictures that flit through his mind, no matter how silly or inconsequential they are. A researcher duly records it all.

Afterwards, the description is compared with the video (and with the other possible video clips which were not chosen). Some of the 'hits', when the receiver has seemed to pick up what the sender is watching on the video, are remarkable.

One sender, for example, was shown a clip from the film *Clash of the Titans*, a scene in which a huge tidal wave engulfs an ancient Greek city containing the statues and columns that we all associate with Greek architecture. People are seen running from the wall of water, which rushed through the buildings. In one shot, people are seen scurrying through a stone tunnel with the water gaining ground on them. There are pictures of debris floating on the flood.

This is what the receiver saw:

'The city of Bath comes to mind. The Romans. The reconstruction of the baths through archaeology. The Parthenon. Also getting sort of buildings like Stonehenge but sort of a cross between Stonehenge and the Parthenon. The Byzantine Empire. The Gates of Thunder. The Holy See. Tables floating about ... The number seven very clearly. That just popped out of nowhere. It reminds me a bit of the first Clash albums. The Clash, 'Two Sevens' I think it was called, I'm not sure ... '

The receiver has picked up the ancient Greek setting, the debris (tables) floating on water, the word Clash from the title of the film, and, interestingly, two sevens. The video clip was ranked as target number seventy-seven by the researchers.

In another test, a sender was shown a newsreel clip of a collapsing bridge, which sways back and forth for some moments before falling from its centre into the water beneath. Lamp-posts on the bridge are seen swaying about.

This is what the receiver picked up:

' . . . something, some vertical object bending or swaying, almost something swaying in the wind . . . Some thin, vertical object bending to the left . . . Some kind of ladder-like structure but it seems to be almost blowing in the wind. Almost like a ladder-like bridge over some chasm that's waving in the wind. This is not vertical, it's horizontal . . . A bridge, a drawbridge over something. It's like one of those old English-type bridges that opens up from either side. The middle part comes up. I see it opening. It's opening. There was a flash of an old, English, stone bridge but then it's back to this one that's opening. The bridge is lifting, both sides now. Now both sides are straight up. Now it's closing again, it's closing, it's coming down, it's closed. Arc, images of arcs, arcs, bridges. Passageways with many arcs, bridges with many arcs . . . '

Here's another one. This time the sender was shown a clip from a film called *Ghost Story*, set in the 1920s. A young blonde is murdered by three young men wearing suits, one wearing a fedora hat with the back pushed up. They kill her by pushing an old car in which she is trapped into a lake. The camera shows their facial expressions as the car sinks. The girl's face and hand appear at the large rectangular window at the back of the car and she can be seen to scream, but no sound is heard. The sequence ends with the car submerged.

This is what the receiver picked up:

' . . . Girl with haircut . . . blonde hair . . . a car . . . The back of someone's head . . . someone running to the right . . . Someone on the right in a brown suit . . . and a fedora hat turned up very much in the back . . . Fedora, trench coat, dark tie . . . A tyre of a car. The car's going to the left. An old movie . . . I'm picturing an Edward G. Robinson movie . . . Big roundish car like 1940s. Those scenes from back window. Bumping once in a while up and down looking through the back window, you see it was probably a big screen in the back of the car and the car's standing still actually . . . I think it's a movie I saw. They're being shot at and shooting at the window and the girl gets shot . . . Girl with a blonde haircut . . . Someone walking in a suit . . . It's the 1940s again, 1930s maybe. Except it looks like it's in colour. Something red, blood . . . blood on someone's lap . . . A dead person all of a sudden. A big mouth opened. Yelling, but no sound . . . Two people running, near a train . . . dressed in 1920s-type suits with balloony pants, like knickers . . . A big old-fashioned white car with a flat top, 1920s, 1930s . . . '

Although the video clips worked better than trying to send still pictures, there were also some strikingly good 'hits' with stills. When a sender looked at a picture of a flying eagle with a white head and black body and outstretched claws, about to land on its perch, this was what the receiver picked up:

' . . . a black bird. I see a dark shape of a black bird with a very pointed beak and his wings down . . . Almost needle-like beak . . . Something that would fly or is flying . . . like a big parrot with long feathers on a perch. Lots of feathers, tail feathers, long, long, long . . . Flying, a big, huge, huge eagle. The wings of an eagle spread out . . . the head of an eagle. White head and dark feathers . . . the bottom of a bird . . .'

The success of ganzfeld research has been repeated often enough to satisfy the scientists that there is a definite improvement in ESP if the receiver is in these specific relaxed conditions (although there are some critics of it, see chapter 7). The success rate also improves if the person sending the image is a friend of the receiver rather than one of the laboratory staff, and if the receiver has tried ganzfeld experiments before (probably because they are more relaxed about the procedures). Crucially for the future of parapsychology, the ganzfeld experiments have demonstrated, more conclusively than any others, that ESP exists and can be measured. The orthodox psychologists, who have rejected parapsychology for years, are beginning to come round. They are impressed not so much by the accuracy of the 'hits' described above, as by the meticulous statistics that Honorton and his colleagues have accumulated to back them. The odds against the recent ganzfield results occurring by chance alone are greater than twenty thousand to one. When analysed with the already existing data from previous ganzfields, the odds are an astronomical ten trillion to one. No longer just a minnow in a fine net of statistics but an enormous whale.

When carried out by experienced researchers in properly controlled conditions, the ganzfield research is as near as parapsychology has come to a repeatable and predictable experiment that demonstrates psi.

Ganzfeld was fathered by another very successful area of parapsychology: dream research. Dream research had a high rate of success. In one series of three hundred and seventy-nine trials, subjects achieved an eighty-three per cent success rate, dreaming about pictures that 'senders' were concentrating on. However, it is an enormously expensive field to work in, staff-intensive and requiring expensive equipment to monitor when sleepers are dreaming. The development of the ganzfeld technique makes very similar research much cheaper and easier.

Laboratory research would be further improved if the parapsychologists could tell beforehand which 'guinea pigs' were going to be good receivers. Unlike other fields of science in which testing is done on human beings, the experimenters do not always need to demonstrate that they are using a representative cross section of the population, because they are not trying to measure the distribution of psi through the population, but only to establish its existence. Being able to pre-select good subjects would be very helpful and the scientists are very close to being able to do this.

First of all, they have established that there is no truth in the old wives' belief that women are more psychic than men. Women may traditionally have been more interested in psi, but there is no evidence that they are better able to experience it, although they are more likely to believe in it. For the last fifty years, scientists have known that whether or not a person believes in psi will affect their scores in ESP experiments. Not only will those who believe do better (and score higher than chance ratings), but those who positively disbelieve will score below chance – a sort of negative psi effect.

The two groups, believers and non-believers, have been labelled sheep and goats. Although up to seventy-five per cent of the population say they believe in some form of ESP, the majority are not clear cut sheep and goats, but are goatish sheep or sheepish goats – a mixture of both sets of belief, but usually coming down noticeably more on one side than the other.

Similarly, extroverts are much more likely to be good psi-testing subjects than introverts. Psychologists Hans Eysenck and Carl Sargent have suggested that this is because ESP experiences in the real world (not the lab) usually involve some communication between people, and a person who is open and gregarious (an extrovert) may be more likely to experience it. This will make them believe in psi, and be more open to psi effects in laboratory testing.

But, as distinguished American parapsychologist Richard Broughton points out, it would be wrong to construe from this that extroverts are more psychic than introverts: it only demonstrates that they are more likely to show psi under test conditions (perhaps introverts are more affected by the lab surroundings, by the unfamiliar researchers and scientists, even by the idea of being tested.)

Although it appears that those who are motivated to do well perform better (the sheep, with a will to reinforce their own beliefs, do better than the goats), trying too hard doesn't work with psi, again confirming that a relaxed attitude is the best one. Some experiments were carried out with subjects who were still being monitored after they were told the tests were over: they all immediately did better when they thought that it no longer counted.

Yet more clues are emerging as to who the good psi performers are. We know that neurotic people are less likely to do well than non-neurotic people – possibly because neurotic people have so much going on inside them that they find the relaxation and opening up that seems to be necessary more difficult. Researchers (among them, the team from Edinburgh University) are now finding that some people are more defensive than others – they can block out and misperceive anything that they see as threatening or arousing (which suggests they could be blocking their own psi abilities). If they are presented with two kinds of words very rapidly, some sexy or violent and the others neutral, they will respond to the neutral ones. More open people will respond to the arousing or threatening words.

'The words are slipped in very fast, so that they cannot easily be detected. Defensive people only pick up that the neutral ones are there, whereas those who are perceptually vigilant will respond to the others.

'If people are defensive, they will essentially defend against psychic material working its way into their awareness. They may do it strongly enough to actually register a negative effect in tests – in other words, they will get a psi test wrong more often than chance would stipulate. Just as some people score well enough for their results to be significant, some score badly enough for their results to be significant, and we call this 'psi-missing'. When we have done more work on this and understand it better it will have implications not just for parapsychology, but within the wider frameworks of industry and daily life,' said Professor Morris.

Young children, particularly those under the age of seven, appear to do well in ESP tests. But there may be reasons for this which are nothing to do with their natural psi ability. For a start, they have not learned to be sceptical – and from the sheep-goat evidence we know that scepticism impairs psi-functioning. They are also likely to be relaxed and happy when taking part in ESP experiments, mainly because researchers take a lot more time and trouble to relax children than they do adults, turning the whole test into a game and taking out of it any sense of being on trial. The children are, in fact, more likely to be in the same frame of mind as the sheep/extroverts – accepting, comfortable and not inhibited.

A more thorough analysis of personality in relation to psi testing has been developed at the Psychophysical Research Laboratories where all guinea pigs have been assessed according to a well-established personality test, the Myers-Briggs Type Indicator which is used in all fields of psychological and sociological research, not specifically parapsychology. According to this test, each person is classified in four ways. There are no rights and wrongs, no classification is better than another, it is simply a way of splitting human personalities into groups.

The first of the four breakdowns is extroversion/introversion. The volunteer is given an E or an I, according to whether they are outward-looking, enjoying action and other people, or inward-looking and detached from those around them. The second classification is perceptual style, which is classified as either sensing or intuitive (S or N). Sensing people prefer concrete and practical matters, intuitives are more at home with abstracts, inferred meanings, hidden possibilities.

The third classification is decision-making and this can be split into thinking or feeling (T or F). Thinkers are good at organization, weigh facts before making decisions, are rational and impartial. Feelers are better at understanding the feelings and points of view of others, they rely on subjective impressions and are concerned with getting on with other people and the effects of decisions on other people. The final category is 'ways of dealing with the outside world', which can be either judging or perceiving (J or P). Judging types are organized and systematic. They lead orderly lives and like to feel in control of their circumstances. Perceiving types are more openminded, they are flexible and go through life trying to adapt to it.

So everyone can be given a four letter evaluation of their personality. (An ISFP, for instance, is an introverted, sensing, feeling, perceptive type.) From this the parapsychologists were able to deduce that not only were extroverts better at ESP tests, so were intuitive types, feeling types and perceptive types, so anyone with an evaluation of ENFP was likely to be a good lab subject. In fact, the combination of feeling and perceptive seemed to be the most important of all, with these people scoring more than twice as well in tests as they could be expected to do by chance.

Another factor which has been found to significantly help psi performance is relaxation: those guinea pigs who have been trained in meditation, yoga or other mental disciplines which teach them to empty their minds are at an advantage when it comes to opening themselves up for ESP.

This large body of information the scientists are accumulating will probably mean that one day we will be able to predict and find 'psi-stars'. Psi-stars are the small group of individuals who seem to have a genuine psychic gift, one that can be tested in the laboratory under the scrutiny of experts and who, time and time again, turn in high-ranking psi scores. Parapsychologists are always delighted to find them, because a psi-star gives them something to get their experimental teeth into. There have been quite a few stars, ranging from those who have remained discreetly as nothing more than a laboratory reference number to those who have accepted and even sought publicity for their skills — with the inevitable result that they have attracted controversy (see chapter 7).

But Professor Morris does not believe that psi abilities are confined to the stars. 'I take an egalitarian approach. There is both anecdotal and experimental evidence that it is not superstar or nothing.'

The Edinburgh researchers have found that their attempts to *improve* the psi-potential of volunteers has not worked. They organized a five-year series of training sessions, at which over two hundred volunteers were taught mental-training techniques and encouraged to practise at home. They found that the participants' psi abilities were not significantly above chance, nor did the results improve from the beginning to the end of each twelve-block training course. There is more research to be done, but the superficial conclusion would seem to be that what you have is what you've got: psi ability is inherent and cannot be created or fostered (even though, as we've seen with ganzfeld, certain conditions will liberate its expression).

On the whole, most laboratories do not recruit their guinea pigs from among the ranks of public stars, or those who have a financial interest in their psi abilities – professional clairvoyants, mediums and the like.

'We stay away from those who use it commercially, or those who attract media attention, because their motivation is suspect,' said Professor Morris. 'We use volunteers, often recruited from evening classes run for members of the public by one of my colleagues. If they've been going to classes, they have some idea what is involved, and they will probably be more relaxed about not finding psi abilities, as well as about finding them.'

So we know which people are likely to be good at ESP tests, and we have a pretty good test to try them on – the ganzfeld. But what about that other great area of laboratory research, psychokinesis? At first sight, PK ought to be easier to deal with and measure. After all, a spoon either bends or it doesn't, a glass either moves across a table on its own or it doesn't. It's not a matter of working out the statistical odds against chance. But, in practice, bending metal and sliding glasses are the province of the 'psi-stars', the exceptional few who appear from time to time and keep the experts buzzing but who are not thick enough on the ground to furnish all the research needs of the parapsychologists. They are rather like the ghosts and the poltergeists: great fun to investigate while they are around, but not a reliable basis for a lifetime's work.

The everyday testing for PK needs to meet the same meticulous statistical demands as the ESP testing and the two areas can overlap. For instance, is predicting the roll of dice precognition or PK? In other words, are you able to see how the dice is going, or are you forcing the dice to go the way you want? So it is important for the scientists to design experiments that do not allow for any confusion about the type of psi being produced though this does not preclude them from being developed along the same lines.

It is important for psi testing to know that the target which the guinea pig is trying to affect or pick up information about is truly random. You can run guessing games with dice and packs of cards at home but the possibilities for fraud, trickery and unconscious help from the person in charge of the experiment are legion, and in the lab these possibilities have to be thoroughly eliminated. Human interference has, as far as possible, to be ruled out while every repetitive lab test has to be interesting and engaging.

One truly random process that the twentieth-century scientists have isolated is radioactive decay. Not only is it unpredictable, but even the hard-headed physicists tell us that it appears to be affected by human consciousness (see chapter 6). Incorporating the decay of a Strontium-90 isotope into a psi-testing machine was the brilliant idea of German-born Helmut Schmidt, who was working at the Boeing Scientific Laboratories in Seattle, Washington, in the 1960s. Not only could he be sure that the guessing game he created for the guinea pigs was random, he was also able to incorporate an automatic recording system which took the drudgery (and the human error) out of constant writing down of results.

The principle of the machine is that as the radioactive material decays, it emits electrons at random intervals. These can be detected by a Geiger counter which registers the emission of the electron and immediately stops an oscillator at any of its cycle of electronic states, causing one of several lights to come on. For ESP testing the subject is asked to predict which light will come on, for PK testing the subject has to try to make the lights obey his or her pattern of choice. Usually the lights are arranged in a circle and the subject has to try to make them light up clockwise or anti-clockwise.

Schmidt even modified the machine to incorporate ESP and PK in the same test, although the guinea pigs were not aware of this. Then he confounded the whole world of parapsychological research by bringing another of the mysteries of modern physics into the equation: time. He pre-recorded tapes of electronic clicks, produced by a refinement of his radioactive random generator, and asked his subjects to listen to them and will them into specific patterns – more weak clicks or more strong clicks. He was not asking them to change the recording (he always kept a copy of each tape) but to influence the random machine that generated the clicks – even though the machine had made the tape days or even weeks earlier. As a control, he kept other sample tapes which were not given to anyone to try to influence. Like his other experiments, it worked: the control tapes showed a random distribution of clicks exactly as chance would predict, the ones that were 'influenced' by the subjects showed results that had odds against happening of one thousand to one.

As a physicist primarily and a parapsychologist second, Schmidt was interested in the developments in quantum mechanics which put the observer back into the system (see chapter 6) and which suggest that human consciousness affects the outcome of sub-atomic reactions.

Schmidt's work has been meticulously carried out and monitored, and other scientists have repeated his experiments. He is not frightened by the critics: he invites them into his laboratory to see how he operates. Unlike some parapsychologists, he does not regard sceptics as the enemy: he sees their cynicism as a yardstick by which to measure himself.

In all, over eight hundred experiments have now been recorded with random generating machines similar to Schmidt's, using sixty-eight independent investigators – ruling out any possibility of fraud. An independent analysis of the results of all these experiments has been carried out and it shows that there is an unequivocal success rate. Because of the rigorous standards he has set in the lab, and because he is happy to work under scrutiny, Schmidt's experiments have done more even than the ganzfeld work to confound the critics.

Psychologist Dr Ray Hyman, a well-respected and highly critical commentator on parapsychology, said about Schmidt:

'By almost any standards, Schmidt's is the most challenging work to confront critics such as myself. His approach makes many of the earlier criticisms of parapsychological research obsolete. [I am] convinced that he was sincere, honest and dedicated to being as scientific as possible . . . the most sophisticated parapsychologist I have ever encountered. If there are flaws in his work they are not the more common or obvious ones.'

Schmidt's is not the only PK research to produce results which stand up to independent scrutiny. William Braud's work at the Mind Science Foundation in San Antonio, Texas, is interesting because it overlaps with psychic healing, a subject which is also technically PK but which is not often tested under lab conditions.

In Braud's main experiments, he and his colleague Marilyn Schlitz tried to help their guinea pigs relax. They deliberately selected a group of people who were emotional, anxious, suffered from ulcers, high blood pressure, tension headaches, and from a room twenty metres away they tried at random intervals to encourage each subject to relax. The degree of relaxation was measured on a polygraph attached to electrodes on the subjects' hands, which recorded the degree of skin resistance.

Thirty-two people were tested, sixteen of them in the high-anxiety group and sixteen controls who were already reasonably relaxed. The subjects were told to make no conscious effort to relax themselves, and were given headphones to listen to random – but not unpleasant – sounds and a screen to watch a randomly changing pattern of coloured squares. Each session lasted twenty-five minutes, and during that time the experimenter would try, at random intervals which he himself had no control over, to encourage relaxation. Braud did this by consciously relaxing himself and visualising the subject relaxing. In the periods when he was not meant to be trying to calm the subject he would try to keep his mind completely off the experiment. Independent assessors could then compare the polygraph readings, showing from the skin readings when the subject was most relaxed, with the graph of the times that attempts were being made to calm the subject.

Since their first experiment ten years ago, there have been twelve more involving over three hundred sessions with two hundred and seventy-one different subjects, and with over sixty people acting as the influencers, trying to relax the subjects (or, as a variation, trying to do the opposite and arouse them). The overall results have been very good, with an odds against chance score of better than forty thousand to one. Obviously, these experiments are more subjective than Schmidt's random generators. There could also be an element of ESP involved, because the subjects could be picking up from the influencers the times at which they wanted them to relax, and could be unconsciously using relaxation techniques on themselves. Nevertheless the reliably good results make this a fruitful area for more work.

There have been hundreds more experiments, many of them yielding extremely promising results. But what makes the ones included here particularly worthy of note is their consistency: they have been tried and tried again, and they come up with the same level of results regularly. All of them have been carefully monitored and fraud or trickery would have to be wholesale, so many different experimenters have been involved.

But what does it all lead to?

As Professor Morris says, we have demonstrated that psi exists, but only as a weak and noisy (unclear) signal. It certainly isn't any use as a regular means of communication. There are claims that some gifted psychics have used their abilities in gambling or in the institutionalized gambling on the Stock Exchange but such stories are apocryphal. Nobody admits to having made a killing with organized psi intelligence, although there are plenty of people who back hunches and play their luck. Unfortunately, their success rate cannot be measured statistically against chance, as the scientists would wish.

It is highly unlikely that in the foreseeable future there will be any way that psi can be harnessed in a reliable way for the good (or otherwise) of society. Remember that even when we are talking about staggeringly high-sounding statistics of success in experiments, the statistics only relate to odds against chance (and anyone who scores seventy out of two hundred and fifty in the five card guessing game has got a one thousand to one success rate. It may be high but seventy out of two hundred and fifty scarcely means that you can rely on the psi).

The parapsychologists have learned a lot about human beings from the laboratory study of psi, and this knowledge is what can bring about the psi pay-off. The final chapter of this book looks at some ways in which psi research can be applied. Many parapsychologists – and Professor Morris in Edinburgh is one – do not believe that we should be studying psi simply to come up with a tidy little experiment which shows some people have telepathy, or whatever. It is part of a much larger framework, an understanding of human beings and society.

'I don't flatter myself or my colleagues that we are going to resolve everything in a scant few years, but I do believe that we are studying something that will come to be regarded as very new. I don't think we are simply learning a bit more about cognitive psychology, or weak bio-physical fields around people, or subjective estimates of probability. We will incidentally learn more about these. But I think it is more than that: I think it is likely that we have access to some means of exchange with our environment that is outside our present understanding.

'If that turns out not to be the case, I won't be knocked off my chair. The world is as it is. It is our job as parapsychologists, just as it is the job of other scientists, to approximate as best we can to a fuller understanding of it.

'The whole history of science is full of ups and downs and reversals and changes in the way we attack things, especially when dealing with concepts at a high level of abstraction. The more you address questions at the top levels of abstraction, the more you have to be prepared for people to find better and better ways to phrase the question. Look at evolutionary theory: after all this time it is still controversial.

'At the lower levels, I feel that we have sufficient good research findings: they cannot easily be dismissed by sophisticated critiques.'

In other words, Professor Morris believes we have sufficient hard evidence to be sure that the paranormal exists. But when it comes to offering theories and hypotheses about it, we've got a long way to go. The laboratory hardware has proved its existence: now we need some explanations. And we won't get them easily.

'Although I'm a believer, I'm still very much a benign sceptic,' said Professor Morris. 'I'm sceptical of anyone who tries to tell me how exactly the world works. I don't think we know. Yet.'

4

Out of Body, Out of Mind

It is impossible to pigeonhole the paranormal. There are a great many disparate events and effects, all worthy of exploration and, where possible, explanation: far too many to cover in a book of this size. This chapter looks at some of the larger areas, where there is an established consistency of experience which makes the subject both better and easier for researchers to study, and more likely to be significant.

Out of Body Experiences

It was a bitterly cold winter's night in the Forth valley in Scotland. Eight-year-old John Lyle was tucked up warm in bed, drowsy and half asleep.

'Suddenly I looked down and saw myself in the bed. I was on the ceiling, watching myself. There was no sense of shock or surprise about it, it felt quite natural. My bedroom was L-shaped and I was at the far end. I could see that the landing light was on, so I moved towards it, along the ceiling. I went into my mother's and father's room and saw them sleeping: I looked down on them from above. Then I moved to the end of the landing where there was a window and I could see car headlights on the road that bent away through the hills.

'After a what seemed like a minute or two I had a very strong feeling that I had to go back to my body, so I went back along the ceiling to my bedroom, and with a small effort of will went down into myself. Although the house was timber-framed and cold in the night, I did not feel cold when I was out of my body. But as I merged back into my body I felt a rush of warmth.'

John's story is a classic out of body experience. Nothing very significant happened and, no doubt, if he had woken his parents to tell them about it they would have dismissed it as a dream. But John knew, with an absolute conviction that has not wavered over the intervening years, that he was not dreaming and that his experience was real. He has no proof, but he is convinced that if something significant had been visible either in his parents' bedroom or in the view from the landing window, he would have seen it because he was there.

Out of body experiences are very common. Surveys have shown that one in six of the population have had them, rising to as many as one in four students (possibly because students are more likely to have used marijuana). Many are as commonplace as John's and don't involve travel outside familiar surroundings. An OBE is not the sort of travel that we are familiar with, the dream travel of our sleep or the fantasy travel of our daydreams. The important difference is that those who have OBEs have a very clear feeling – as strong as a knowledge – that they have left their own bodies behind and can look down on them objectively. Most OBEs happen spontaneously, usually, though not always, while the subject is very relaxed (there is one report of a girl sitting on the roof of the car while she was taking her driving test!). Others are prompted by unusual circumstances: a substantial proportion happen when a person is in hospital, or is ill. Typically, they may be able to see themselves being treated, even hear in detail the conversations being held about them, although they are unconscious and not experiencing any pain.

A survey of people who have had OBEs shows that seventy-eight per cent occurred when the subject was very relaxed; fifteen per cent were unusually fatigued; eight per cent were using a drug; six per cent were under anaesthetic; nine per cent were in an active situation (for instance, having sexual intercourse); twenty-two per cent reported that they were under exceptional stress at the time.

In some OBEs the subject is very aware of having a second body which looks and behaves very much like the first one and may not even have the capacity to travel except by normal human means like walking. But in most cases the subject is comparatively unaware of their second body and has instead a sensation of the self leaving the physical body and floating away. Some report having no body at all, but simply a viewpoint outside themselves; others feel they are an amorphous shape, or a source of light. Others accept the existence of a body, without examining it. (Some subjects talk about the clothes they wear, which are almost always the same as the ones their 'real' body is wearing.)

There are certain characteristics that seem to be common to the majority of OBEs: vision is better than normal (seeing with 'great clarity' is often referred to in OBE reports) and even at night the scene is infused by a soft light. Physical objects, such as walls and furniture can either be seen or passed through with natural ease. The sensation of floating is enjoyable, although, like John Lyle, a lot of subjects feel a strong need to get back to their bodies. Attempts to pick things up, to write, or to make others in the room aware of their disembodied presence all fail. Even reading is reported to be much more difficult than is usual. The ability to have OBEs is not restricted to a particular group: men and women, young and old, rich and poor, educated and uneducated all appear to have the same chance of having one. Religious belief does not seem to influence the likelihood either. One of the few things that does appear to induce them is drugs, especially marijuana.

Out of body experiences have a very long pedigree, having been reported in some form or other since records of civilization began. In primitive cultures, OBEs are often an accepted part of the armoury of the shaman or medicine man. He would be required to 'travel' to distant places to check up on the activities of other tribes, to alert the village to visitors on their way, to spy out where to hunt for game.

There are plenty of historical and legendary references to

OBEs. When the King of Syria wondered how the Israelites seemed to be able to anticipate his plans and suspected that they had planted a spy, he was told that the 'spy' was the prophet Elisha, who was able to leave his body behind in Israel and visit the King's bedchamber where plans were being laid.

Usually the OBE only affects the person having it who travels invisibly. Occasionally, however, they are seen by others at the place they visit. The most famous example is that of an Italian monk, Alphonsus Liguori, the founder of the Redemptorist Order, who fell into a trance while celebrating mass at Amalfi in 1774. When he woke up he assured everyone that he had been in Rome at the bedside of the dying Pope Clement XIV. A few days later, news reached Amalfi that he had indeed been there and had been seen by many witnesses. In the 1840s, a French schoolteacher was sacked from her post because the girls at the school were so upset by constantly seeing her in two places at once, often standing or sitting side by side herself. In recent times, Indian swamis have been seen in two places at once. One, Dadaji, seems to have been able to eat, drink and smoke cigarettes in both places. Of course, all these stories carry the usual anecdotal risks: when details are not reported until sometime afterwards it is impossible to be sure that the timings were right. More commonly, those at the scene of the visit do not see the person having the OBE but report sensing a presence.

Early research into OBEs was prompted by the same question that sparked a lot of psychical research: does separation from the physical body prove that human beings have a soul independent of their earthly shell and, if so, does this prove that there is life after death? Some Eastern religions encompass the idea of another body in the afterlife, rather than just a soul, and Spiritualists believe that on the next level of existence after death we will all look and behave very much as we do physically in this world.

The Theosophical movement, which fell into disarray after its founder, Madame Blavatsky, was exposed as a fraud (see chapter 1) but which survived and is still in existence today, promulgated the idea of 'astral bodies'. An amalgam of different Eastern doctrines, essentially, Theosophy claims that we all have many different bodies, each finer than the one below it. Our coarse human bodies are the lowest of the low, but each of us has a physical double, another body that is firmly attached to the one we see when we look in the mirror. This extra body, known as an 'etheric' body, is our link with our higher bodies and it seldom leaves us except at times of great crisis or near death. There is another body, however, the 'astral' body, which is one more stage up the ladder and which can separate from the physical body. The astral body is the seat of consciousness and senses so, when the physical body is left behind, it is from the astral body that things are seen and felt. According to this doctrine, astral bodies leave the physical body during sleep and roam around in a disorganised way which is not remembered when awake. Theosophists believe it is possible to be trained to remember, however, and to control the travel of the astral body.

In a few descriptions of OBEs, subjects talk about seeing a cord trailing back from their second body to the first. This fits in with later Theosophical teaching which says that a silver cord links the two and if it is severed it causes death. But the vast majority of OBE reports do not involve a cord. Early work on OBEs was mostly confined to the anecdotal reports, but some researchers did try to check out and get corroboration for information that was picked up while out of the body. Obviously, the acid test of the reality of the experience is whether or not it provided knowledge that could not have been acquired without travelling to the OBE destination while, at the same time, there is corresponding proof that the physical body stayed in one place. One excellent example reported in 1963 came from a woman who was seriously ill with peritonitis and was in bed in hospital. The ward was L-shaped, and as she lay there she could not see round the corner.

'One morning, I felt myself floating upwards and found I was looking down on the rest of the patients. I could see myself propped up against the pillows, very white and ill. I saw the sister and nurse rush to my bed with oxygen. Then everything went blank. The next I remember was opening my eyes to see the sister bending over me. I told her what had happened and, at first, she thought I was rambling. Then I said: "There is a big woman sitting up in bed with her head wrapped in bandages and she is knitting something with blue wool. She has a very red face." This certainly shook her, as apparently the lady concerned had had a mastoid operation and looked just as I described. She was not allowed out of bed and, of course, I hadn't been up at all. After I'd given her several other details, such as the time by the clock on the wall (which had broken down) I convinced her that something strange had happened to me, at least.'

There are many problems investigating such stories. Often the researcher hears about them too late to track down witnesses and there is the acknowledged risk of the memory playing tricks: facts can unconsciously be embellished or changed to make them fit the rehearsed story. The more it's told, the better it gets. As the vast majority of people who have OBEs have only one, or possibly two, in a lifetime, it is impossible to be on hand with notebook and pen to record all the details at the time.

There are another group of people who have opened the door to serious research of OBEs: the small band who do have them regularly. John Lyle is now in his forties and is resolutely cynical about the paranormal but, ever since that night in his childhood, he has sensed the ability to repeat his out of body experience should he choose to.

'Something very deep in myself seems to warn me against doing so, and I have never tried. But once or twice I have been aware of positively restraining myself from slipping out of my body again,' he says.

It does appear to be true that some people are able to take off on such journeys more or less at will. These are the people who are in the best position to provide researchers with proof. One-off OBEs occasionally come up with startling and irrefutable facts to support them but most are, like John Lyle's, a matter of nothing more than a deep personal conviction that this was no ordinary dream experience. Even if the proof exists, it will rarely satisfy scientific standards.

Any serious research into the nature and cause of OBEs has to be carried out with those who can trigger them fairly reliably. These OBE adepts are usually able to travel farther afield than those who experience spontaneous OBEs, which makes it easier to test them for knowledge of places outside their familiar surroundings. The problem that arises in controlled experiments comes when establishing the difference between what the subject has seen while having an OBE and what he has seen clairvoyantly. He himself may find it hard to detect a difference and much of the research done has proved inconclusive: even with elaborate screens set around objects in order to hide them from the general view provided by clairvoyance but enabling them to be seen by a subject who could move around to the right position (OBE).

Californian parapsychologist Charles Tart tested one young woman by asking her, while she was out of her body, to remember a number that was written on a piece of card on top of a cupboard. It could not be seen from normal eye level. The woman slept in the laboratory for four nights. On the first, she had no OBE. On the next, she was not able to get high enough to see the card. On the third night, she travelled away from the laboratory and did not attempt to see the card. Finally, on the fourth night, she remembered the five-digit number, 25132, perfectly. He was unable to carry out any further experiments with her and did not feel he had completely excluded cheating (although he thought it very unlikely). But it was also possible that the woman had been able to use ESP.

A similar experiment was carried out with the psi-star Ingo Swann, who was able to have OBEs more or less at will. He identified correctly various target objects on a platform suspended from the ceiling. Not all of his drawings of the objects were perfect but a judge correctly matched them to the targets. Again, the problem is one of knowing how he acquired the information, whether by clairvoyance or when having an OBE. Attempts to try to sort out this problem physiologically, by showing that brain wave activity is different during OBEs, have been inconclusive but what has been established is that OBEs do not happen during dreams: they are definitely not an unusual type of dream. (It is possible to know when someone is dreaming by recording their different types of sleep. REM sleep, or rapid eye movement sleep, is the dream state, easily identified because the eyes move rapidly. It happens about every ninety minutes during a normal night's sleep, each dream lasting longer than the preceding one, so that they vary from a few minutes to half an hour.)

Approaching the problem from the other end, by trying to find out if the OBE subject could be detected at the place he was visiting, seems to have provided better proof. Keith 'Blue' Harary was found to be a gifted psychic while he was a student at Duke University in North Carolina. He was able to have OBEs at will, and the parapsychologists at the university were quick to capitalize on this discovery by planning experiments around him.

In one, he was asked to visit a room where a kitten was being monitored by researchers. The kitten, which was fond of Harary, seemed to settle down and be far more contented whenever he was 'visiting' the room. All the proper controls were in place, so that the researchers in the room did not know when he was going to be with them. During eight sample periods when Harary was not visiting, the kitten miaowed thirty-seven times and wandered about its enclosure. When he was 'there' it did not miaow once.

In the 1960s an American businessman, Robert Monroe, discovered that he was able to have OBEs at will and, after an initial period of worry during which his doctor checked him over and found nothing wrong with him, he tried to harness the experiences. On one occasion, he 'went' to visit a friend who had been ill and was surprised to see the man outside his house with his wife. When he checked with them later, it transpired that they *had* been outside: his friend was feeling better and had gone out for a breath of fresh air. Monroe was even able to describe the clothes they were both wearing. Some details were wrong, however. The friend did not speak the words that Monroe heard him say. This mixture of correct and incorrect details is typical of most OBEs.

Monroe was tested in the laboratory, but without a great deal of success. However, when Charles Tart, who had been testing him, moved to California, the two of them agreed on an informal experiment. It was agreed that on a certain night, Tart and his wife would try to help Monroe have an OBE and come to their home, which he had never seen. Tart gave him no further details. At 11 p.m., when it would be 2 a.m. in Virginia where Monroe lived, Tart and his wife started to concentrate on inducing the OBE. Five minutes later, their phone rang but they ignored it in order not to break their concentration.

The following day they found that it was Monroe who had phoned them at 11.05 p.m.. He said he had taken an out of body trip, assisted by someone who had held his wrist. He had drifted down into a room, and, when he 'returned' to his own home, rang Tart immediately. His description of the room, of the number of people there, and of what Tart and his wife were doing contained a lot of inaccuracies: none the less the timing had been accurate.

The experts are divided on the question of whether OBEs constitute paranormal experiences or can be explained by orthodox psychology. It is easier to explain rationally (and non-paranormally) OBEs that stay close to the body when, for instance, the person seems to hover above their own body but does not travel away from it, as in the typical hospital scene. Psychologists believe these could be a special kind of hallucination, based on memory and on the information that is getting through to the brain despite the lack of consciousness. Psychologist Dr Susan Blackmore, who has studied OBEs, believes they are caused by a temporary hiccup in the way we perceive the world around us.

'We build a model of the world as though we are sitting

in our heads looking out but that is only a convenient model for us to use when we are functioning normally. The computer that is the brain builds that model: it could equally build a model based on looking from the ceiling. When we are in pain or crisis, or are semi-conscious, the brain may pick an alternative viewpoint because it is the best available at the time, when the normal sources of information – our senses – are disrupted.'

She describes it as the brain's 'best guess' at a view of the world, when the normal information channels are not working. So the view is built from memory, which accounts for the familiar surroundings. 'Everything perceived in an OBE is a product of memory and imagination,' she says in her book, *Beyond the Body*. 'During the OBE, one's own imagination is more vividly experienced than it is in everyday life. In other words, the experience is a kind of privileged peek into the contents of one's own mind.'

The weakness with the theory is that it does not satisfactorily explain the way that OBE subjects can pick up information they could not otherwise have known. The suggestion from other researchers that this knowledge is gained using ESP has not been either proven or disproven. (Proof of ESP itself is not exactly plentiful and what facts there are suggest that it is erratic and unpredictable.) Some OBE research – for example, with the kitten – would suggest that an OBE is a unique and individual phenomenon.

Lucid Dreaming

Lucid dreaming follows naturally from OBEs, not because the two things are the same (one of the few things we know about OBEs is that they do not take place when the subjects are dreaming), but because they do have some similar characteristics.

A lucid dream is one in which the dreamer is aware that he is dreaming and can, to a large extent, control and direct the dream. Although it does not have the same strong sense of reality as an OBE, it feels natural and normal. A common feature of a lucid dream is that the subject realizes he is dreaming when something preposterous and dream-like happens and he says to himself, 'It's OK because it's only a dream,' and can then go on with the action in the full, clear knowledge that he is dreaming.

As with OBEs, many people have the occasional lucid dream. However it seems to be possible for anyone to train themselves to have a lucid dream although it can take years of practice. (One of the early psychic researchers, F.W.H. Myers, tried for three thousand nights and only managed three lucid dreams.) The main route to lucid dreaming appears to be keeping a dream diary: consistently writing down the details of dreams on waking. One's memory of one's dreams improves rapidly from only a few scraps of detail until, within a few weeks, large dream sequences can be remembered. Making the leap from this stage to lucid dreaming is difficult, but suggested ways include examining your dreams and concentrating on the absurd elements of them (as this seems to be a common way, during the dream, of realizing that it is one) and creating dream scenarios for yourself in the last few moments of drowsy consciousness before falling asleep. Myers seems to have been particularly unlucky: most people who set out to have lucid dreams report that they are quite successful.

Why should anyone want lucid dreams?

Sheer pleasure, for a start. Here are a couple of dreams reported to psychologist Dr Keith Hearne, who has specialized in the study of them and whose book, *The Dream Machine*, surveys the whole field of lucid dreaming.

'I went for a walk within my old school as I remembered it. A tennis teacher asked me to wait, as I passed the courts. She ran up and kissed me. I was certain that this, being too good to be true, would waken me, but it did not. She was wearing a white skirt and singlet, with white socks and plimsolls. She pulled me down on top of her onto the grass. I remember the people were walking past and took no notice of us . . . '

In his dream, the sleeper went on to make love, very enjoyably, to the teacher. Other lucid dreamers have told

Dr Hearne about having sex with pop stars, ex-lovers and strangers. Several of his subjects have told him that when they realize they are dreaming lucidly they deliberately engineer sexual situations. Others find a different kind of satisfaction: one fifteen-year-old created a situation in his dream in which he beat up a school bully.

But are lucid dreams part of the paranormal? Or are they simply a refined version of the everynight dreams we all need to keep our brains ticking over?

Forty per cent of all psychic phenomena reported by the general public involves premonitions, and more than half of these premonitions occur in dreams. Almost all the evidence is anecdotal, although Hearne did experiment with one woman who was able to dream lucidly and who had a history of having precognitive dreams of major world events (for instance, the assassination of President Sadat and the attempt on the life of President Reagan). To avoid the criticism that only the successful dreams are recorded and the unsuccessful ones are forgotten, Hearne kept a record of all her premonitory dreams for a year, fifty-two in all. They were then blind-judged against newspaper reports for the year, while controls looked at other years' news reports. There was slight evidence that she had predicted events, but not enough to be statistically significant.

Evidence for ESP in lucid dreams is almost all anecdotal and not as strong as the evidence for OBEs. Oliver Fox, one of the early pioneers of OBE study, had a lucid dream in which he read two questions from an examination paper he was due to sit, although he found the process of reading in his dream difficult. One of Hearne's subjects reported a dream in which he was at a friend's house and, when he later compared notes with the friend, some of the things he saw and the time at which he dreamed of them corresponded with reality.

Hearne tried experiments with subjects who signalled to him that they were dreaming lucidly. He picked up a number at random and stared at it. The subjects had been told beforehand that he would be doing this and their dreams did consistently feature lots of numbers but rarely the right one. The 'numbers' theme may well have been triggered because they knew in advance that Hearne would be selecting a number, rather than because the number itself was communicated in any way to them.

Near Death Experiences

'I was floating up out of my body. I did not know how I got there. I was going somewhere where I was much happier. It was totally peaceful. Indeed, it was wonderful to see what it is like up there.

'I could see what happens in the next world. I saw loved ones who had long since died, especially my mother who died when I was only five years old. I don't remember how it ended, because somebody up there said: "We don't think we want you yet." It wasn't a voice, more a feeling. But I do know that now I am not frightened of death.'

This is the description given by the Marquis of Tavistock, heir to the Duke of Bedford's estate, of an experience he had when he came close to death. In February 1988, when he was forty-nine, Robin Tavistock, who runs the 13,000-acre Woburn Estate with its famous Safari Park, suffered a massive stroke. After a major brain operation, surgeons gave him only a one per cent chance of survival. It was during those first critical six hours that he believes he went out of his body and into the life after death which he is now convinced awaits him at the end of life. After a valiant and difficult struggle, he is now almost completely recovered from the stroke that left him temporarily paralysed, speechless and incontinent. But, in other ways, he is permanently changed: more philosophical, less tense, more able to enjoy life.

Near Death Experiences have been reported for centuries and the Marquis of Tavistock's has many of the hallmarks of a typical one. There are more today than ever before: probably because medical science is better able to rescue people from the brink of death, often after they have stopped breathing and even after their brains have almost stopped functioning. But not everyone who nearly dies has the experience. Various surveys of those who have survived acute life-threatening situations in hospitals have found that only about half of them have had NDEs. But the experience is common enough for a society to have been founded in America, the International Association for Near Death Studies.

One thing that distinguishes an NDE from an out of body experience (apart from timing) is the pattern that seems to run through NDEs. Whereas OBEs and lucid dreams take many forms, almost all NDEs follow an established track. An American doctor, Raymond Moody, studied NDEs in the 1970s, as part of a drive to help people overcome their fear of death by talking about it. He compiled a 'typical' NDE: while acknowledging that none of the stories he heard from patients matched this account in all details, features of it were common to all.

'A man is dying and, as he reaches the point of greatest physical distress, he hears himself pronounced dead by his doctor. He begins to hear an uncomfortable noise, a loud ringing or buzzing, and at the same time feels himself moving very rapidly through a long dark tunnel. After this, he suddenly finds himself outside his own physical body but still in the same immediate physical environment and he sees his own body from a distance, as though he was a spectator. He watches the resuscitation attempt from his vantage point and is in a state of emotional upheaval.

'After a while, he collects himself and becomes more accustomed to his odd condition. He notices that he still has a "body", but one of a very different nature and with very different powers from the physical body he has left behind. Soon other things begin to happen. Others come to meet and to help him. He glimpses the spirits of relatives and friends who have already died and a loving, warm spirit of a kind he has never encountered before – a being of light – appears before him. This being asks him questions, non-verbally, to make him evaluate his life and helps him along by showing him a panoramic instantaneous playback of the major events of his life. At some point he finds himself approaching some sort of barrier or border, apparently representing the limit between earthly life and the next life. Yet he finds that he must go back to earth, that the time for his death has not yet come. At this point he resists, for by now he is taken up with his experiences of the afterlife and does not want to return. He is overwhelmed by intense feelings of joy, love and peace. Despite his attitude, though, he somehow reunites with his physical body and lives . . . The experience affects his life profoundly, especially his views about death and its relationship to life.'

Many subjects experience only the early part of this scenario, although a few seem to skip earlier sections and go on to the later stages. Psychologist Kenneth Ring outlined five stages: the first is a feeling of great peace and well being; the second is a separation from the physical body; the third is going into darkness or a tunnel; the fourth is seeing the light and the fifth is passing into the light.

One common factor in all studies of NDEs is that they seem to be very pleasant experiences: there are hardly any reports of subjects going to hell or purgatory and a reluctance to return to their physical bodies characterizes many of them. Some subjects tell of being sent back to their bodies, others of asking to go back – usually for some pressing unfinished business, like bringing up a family. Often, in the OBE stage, the subject hears those around his physical body talking and is sometimes able to report to doctors and nurses afterwards exactly what they said as they tried to revive him. At the stage at which they meet dead relatives, some subjects have been able to bring back with them tales of seeing people who they did not know were dead but are subsequently found to be so. What's more, these near death experiences coincide very closely with what we know of death experiences. The words spoken and descriptions given by patients who subsequently die some moments later seem to tally with those reported by death survivors. Research into deathbed visions and hallucinations in the late 1950s and early 1960s led to a questionnaire being sent out to five hundred doctors and five thousand nurses in America, asking them to record what they had heard at the bedsides of dying patients.

Uniformly, their reports suggested that the mood of the patients lifted dramatically and descriptions of angels and dead relatives were common. A scene of indescribable beauty was another regular component. In 1977, an important survey was published, giving the results of a comparison between the experiences of the dying in the USA and India. It was an attempt to establish whether the visions the dying patient reported to his doctors and nurses varied across cultures. If they varied enormously, it could be construed that they were visions created within the patient's collapsing brain and their content the result of the cultural and religious expectations of the patient. If they proved to be substantially the same regardless of background and creed, it could be taken that they were reports of something which existed outside the patient, possibly an afterlife. The medical staff were asked to record details of the patients' beliefs, drugs they were taking and the nature of their illness as well as noting changes in their moods and, as fully as possible, the story that they told.

Although there is no foolproof way of assessing this kind of information (the medical staff may, unwittingly, inject their own input into the details; their memories may not be reliable; and, the factor that is most likely to distort statistics, those who reply to such a survey are going to be only those who have something to report), none the less the survey was sufficiently wide-ranging to be of some significance. There were, in fact, few differences between the two groups, one predominantly Christian and the other almost exclusively Hindu, despite the cultural and religious gulf separating them. Eighty per cent of all visions reported were of dead people or religious figures, with the Hindus reporting more religious visions. In both groups over ninety per cent of the dead people seen in the visions were relatives of the patient and sixty-five per cent felt that this person had come to take them away. One of the few differences was that the Hindus were more reluctant to go, those raised in a Christian tradition more serene and accepting of the transition from life. This survey and others have shown that drugs appear to have little or no impact on the likelihood or the nature of deathbed visions. The consistency of the findings led the two parapsychologists who carried out the research, Karlis Osis and Erlendur Haraldsson, to conclude that they have found evidence that there is life after death.

There have been attempts to explain NDEs scientifically, most notably by psychologist Dr Susan Blackmore, who works at Bath and Bristol universities. She believes the tunnel effect that occurs in many NDEs is caused by the brain being starved of oxygen. 'The inhibitory cells in the brain die first and the excitable ones take longer to die. In the visual system many cells are packed into the centre and they thin out towards the edge. The excitable ones are all firing like mad, in a hyperactive way, and because there are masses and masses at the centre and less at the side, it looks like a big bright light. As the light gets bigger, you get the illusion of travelling along the tunnel (just as you do when the train on the platform next to yours starts to move).'

Dr Blackmore acknowledges that her theory only encompasses a small part of the near death experience and a part that is not common to all. If her physiological explanation is true, then it must cross all cultural boundaries. She is currently checking a report which says that although Indians have NDEs, they do not report travelling through tunnels. By and large, though, the tunnel effect does appear to be ubiquitous.

Other researchers regard the NDE as nothing more than a hallucination, caused by the brain being deprived of oxygen. But NDEs defy classification as hallucinations because of their very uniformity. Hallucinations are chaotic, unpredictable, varied from one subject to another. The cultural acceptance of 'heaven' and an afterlife in which the newly-dead are reunited with their long-dead relatives and friends is not strong enough to account for the prevalence of this scenario. As Dr Blackmore has discovered interviewing people who have survived close encounters with death, the distribution of NDEs is a lottery. Strong religious believers are no more likely to have them than those with little or no commitment to religion. And the lack of oxygen theory can also be challenged by the fact that NDEs are reported by people who have not experienced lack of oxygen. There have been reports of NDEs from subjects anticipating their own death while falling off a cliff. At the moment of falling their brains were not deprived of oxygen, but they report very similar NDEs to subjects suffering massive cardiac arrest.

Almost all those who have NDEs find them enormously beneficial experiences. They lose their fear of death, they appreciate life more, their beliefs in an afterlife are enhanced. Whether they are, in fact, travellers who have returned from the bourn of Hamlet's undiscovered country and whether or not their experiences should reassure us all as to the nature of that country, we do not know. What we do know is that so far no adequate explanation can rationalize their experiences away.

Crisis Visions

Crisis visions are another common phenomenon cited as proof that we survive the death of our bodies. Since the earliest studies of ghosts and apparitions, it has been clear that a disproportionate number involve visions of people who are dying. In other words, a subject clearly sees an apparition of a relative or friend, only to discover later that the moment they saw it was the moment the person died. Sometimes the vision comes within a few hours either side of the death, sometimes the vision is not of someone who dies but of someone who is none the less in great crisis, having just suffered an accident, for instance. For purposes of analysis, we lump all these together as crisis visions and have set a cut-off point at twelve hours either side of the moment of crisis. (This rather arbitrary point was reached originally by Edmund Gurney, whose massive survey of ghosts and apparitions, *Phantasms of the Living*, was published in 1886.)

'I woke suddenly in the middle of the night. I felt unnaturally hot and I was perspiring. As I sat up to get some air I was aware of a figure sitting on the end of the bed. It took me a few moments to recognize my mother's cousin Anthony. I had not seen him for many years: he lived in Wales and I was in London, and my family had never been close to his. For a spell during my childhood, when I was about twelve and his own marriage had just broken up, he had stayed with my parents. I think he stayed for about three or four months. I was his favourite. I was the only girl in the family and he spoiled me with sweets and presents. When he moved back to his native Wales, I wrote to him for a while but as I grew older, went to university, got married, had my own family, all those things got in the way.

'I knew he was a lonely old man towards the end of his life and, whenever I thought about him, which was only occasionally, I felt I should sit down and write a long letter but I somehow never got round to it. As I saw him sitting on the end of my bed, I imagined there was a reproachful look on his face and I made up my mind to write to him the next day. I did not feel at all threatened or frightened by his presence, but I knew very clearly that I was not dreaming and that he was really there. He did not speak. I turned to wake my husband and when I turned back my uncle was gone. I told my husband what I had seen and the next afternoon I wrote a letter. That evening my mother rang to say she had heard from an aunt in Wales that Anthony had died the night before at about 4 a.m. It was a quarter to five when I woke my husband. My husband and the letter, written before the phone call, are testimony to the reality of my vision.'

This is a typical crisis vision, with at least some corroboration (from the husband) that the young woman saw the vision before she knew of her uncle's death and that the time of death corresponded roughly with the time of the vision.

Crisis visions of the dying account for about fourteen per cent of all sightings of apparitions and the percentage is higher if it includes those who do not die but are in some other kind of crisis, physical, mental or emotional, at the time they appear to a friend or relative. In eighty-five per cent of all crisis visions the person having the apparition has no idea that the person they see is about to die and in half of all cases the vision is seen within half an hour of the known time of death. These statistics are taken from a survey by Erlendur Haraldsson, an Icelandic parapsychologist, and were published in 1991. They confirm the conclusions of other surveys, including one done a hundred years ago by the SPR. It seems that crisis visions are a constant and not uncommon part of human experience – one in twenty people can expect to have the experience at some time in their lives.

Not only are they relatively common, but of all spontaneous psychic phenomena they are, according to Professor Bob Morris, 'the most difficult to rationalize away'. Professor Morris carried out an informal study with students he was teaching in America. He asked them all to find from among their friends and relatives a story of the paranormal, part of the anecdotal evidence that belongs in every family's folklore. Then he asked them to apply themselves seriously to working out the possible rational or non-paranormal explanations for the story.

'Many were so lacking in detail it was impossible to do much with them. But many others could, with a little bit of analysis, be ascribed to probability, or to some extraneous physical effect, or to forgotten memories and so on. The core of cases for which explanations were most difficult to come by were the crisis visions,' he explained.

Not all crisis phenomena are apparitions. Sometimes the recipient hears the voice of the dying person, often calling their name. In a major survey in America by Louisa Rhine this was the largest group of cases. In 1907 a Frenchwoman, living in Bordeaux, reported being woken by a voice calling her name, Jeanne, three times as if in agony. She later learned that her former fiancé, who had been prevented from marrying her, had died that night and had called her name out on his deathbed. In other auditory cases there are no voices, only sounds – although often sounds associated with the dead person.

Occasionally the vision is both seen and heard. Playwright David Belasco was moved to write *The Return of Peter Grimm*, which deals with the paranormal, after seeing his mother in his bedroom and hearing her voice calling 'Davy, Davy, Davy', his childhood name. A few hours later, he learnt that she died 'at about the time that I saw her in my room. Later, I learned that just before she died she roused herself, smiled and three times murmured "Davy".'

Sometimes there is something other than sight or sound involved: the recipient experiences pain or, perhaps, great warmth or coldness, which corresponds to the condition of the dying person. Among her collection of cases, Dr Rhine has the story of a schoolteacher who was caring for her elderly mother and aunt.

'Shortly after I arrived at the school where I teach I went into the office. Suddenly an extremely severe pain struck my shoulder and chest, so intense that it made me cry out . . . About an hour after this I had a call. My aunt had suffered a heart attack as she and my mother were going downstairs. She had died instantly, with only my mother there. As well as we could estimate, it had happened about the time the severe pain had struck me.'

There are many stories of events that happen to coincide with the time of death, but which do not directly affect any other human being. There are dogs which howled when their masters, away at war, were killed. There are pictures that fell off walls and, particularly, clocks that stopped. Everyone knows the song about the grandfather clock which 'stopped, dead, never to go again, when the old man died'. The problem with so much anecdotal evidence is that the coincidence of dates and times gets improved in the telling: the grandfather clock may have stopped, quite naturally, some time around the day of death, but it will be remembered as spot-on timing.

Can there be an explanation for crisis visions or crisis communications? When the early SPR researchers noted the frequency with which crisis visions occurred, they assumed that they had strong evidence of an afterlife. This has been challenged by those who believe the visions are hallucinations, combined with (or prompted by) telepathy or clairvoyance. In other words, a telepathic or clairvoyant communication with the dying person alerts the recipient to the crisis and the strong emotion this generates contributes to them hallucinating about their relative or friend. The late Brian Nisbet, who was a member of the SPR for many years, summed it up: 'It may be that, at unconscious level, we are more in touch with each other than we realize consciously and that this contact is there even after death. At present, we do not know enough about the human psyche or the extent and limitations of unconscious processes to give a definite answer.'

Coincidences

When the author Russell Lewis was writing his novel, *Lip Service*, he opened one chapter with a quotation from playwright Tom Stoppard: 'One of the things that make novels less plausible than history, I find, is the way they shrink from coincidence.' Lewis had no idea, as he typed the words, that his whole book was a framework of coincidences with the life of a woman he had never met, yet with whom he had a connection.

When the book was published in January 1991, Lewis gave a copy to his friend Tim Hopkins, who read it with growing surprise. The life of the novel's heroine bore a strong resemblance to the life of Hopkins's mother, although the two men had never discussed her, Lewis had never met her and knew nothing of her background. The central female character in the book is Hungarian and she settles in the Crystal Palace area of London on her arrival in England. Hopkins's mother lived in the Crystal Palace area when she first moved to London and, although she is not Hungarian, her second husband was. His Christian name was Gabor; in the book, the heroine's surname is Gabor. Both women have a sister called Polly. In the book, the heroine has a friend called Ada, while in real life Ada is the name of the woman's mother. The heroine in the book is called Maya, in real life there is another sister called May.

Both the real and the fictional woman have a close friendship with a yoga-practising, vegetarian Hindu. Both women are Communists, and both make pilgrimages to Highgate cemetery with their sons to visit the grave of Karl Marx.

'Both Russell Lewis and I are sceptics,' said Tim Hopkins. 'Still, we were both confounded by the number of similarities. My mother is a Spiritualist and so is Russell's, another coincidence that we did not discover until we talked about the book. My mother has read the book and, although a bit alarmed at the sexual frankness in it, she, too, is astonished by the parallels with her life and has suggested that Russell somehow acquired the information telepathically from me.'

Another, even more striking, example of how life and art can mimic each other is Morgan Robertson's book *Futility*, which was published in 1898. It is about the building of a great liner called the *Titan*, which on a voyage in April struck an iceberg and sank. Fourteen years later, on 14 April 1912, the *Titanic* went down. Both boats were constructed around the principle of water-tight compartments which were believed to make them unsinkable. Both were carrying too few lifeboats, both tragedies resulted in appalling loss of life. In his book, Robertson gave precise details about the ship: 3,000 people on board (the Titanic was carrying 2,207); 24 lifeboats (the Titanic had 20); the speed at time of impact of 25 knots (23 knots); displacement tonnage 75,000 (66,000); length 800 feet (882.5 feet); number of propellers 3 (3).

Coincidences are the root of many people's beliefs in the paranormal. While, as Tom Stoppard suggests, most people underestimate the frequency of coincidences in life (see chapter 7), on the other hand, some coincidences are so complex and contain so many parallels that it is hard not to read significance into them and see them as examples of at least telepathy or precognition, if not as a phenomenon in their own right. Carl Gustav Jung, the famous psychiatrist and psychotherapist, coined the word 'synchronicity' for coincidences (they are events that are in some way synchronized, though apparently unconnected). He became sidetracked in the search for synchronicity in horoscopes: his research was later proved to be heavily biased towards finding the results he was seeking among star signs and has been subsumed by the controversy surrounding astrology.

Jung believed that two or more coincidences which appear to be causally unlinked will, in fact, be related to each other in meaning. To understand this link, it is necessary to believe in a 'collective unconscious': a store of memories and knowledge shared by every human being but only accessible at times of heightened emotion or in the particular physical conditions which we cannot yet instigate at will. His theories have been better expressed by psychologist Robert Aziz, who says there are four types of meaning that can be found in a coincidence: the fact of the psychic state and the physical event paralleling each other; the emotional charge that results from realizing the coincidence; the subjective meaning of the coincidence (how the person it affects interprets it within his own life) and the objective interpretation (how it fits in with the idea of an underlying store of common memories in mankind). One of Jung's favourite examples of coincidence occurred when he was with a patient who was telling him about her dream of being given a golden scarab (a beetle of great symbolic value in ancient Egypt).

'While she was telling me this dream, I sat with my back to the closed window,' Jung wrote. 'Suddenly, I heard a noise behind me, like a gentle tapping. I turned round and saw a flying insect knocking against the window pane from outside. I opened the window and caught the creature in the air as it flew in. It was the nearest analogy to a golden scarab that one finds in our latitudes, a scarabaeid beetle, which contrary to its usual habits had evidently felt an urge to get into a darkened room at this particular moment.'

It was this story, reinforced by an incident they shared, that prompted David Curtis and Roderick Main, two

British researchers, to call their project researching into the meaningfulness of coincidences Scarab Research. The two of them had been discussing their interest in coincidences with a mutual friend as they walked along the banks of the Isis in Oxford. As the friend turned to leave them he noticed an insect on his trouser leg: it was a scarabaeid beetle.

Main, who is a postgraduate student working on the psychology of religion, believes that coincidences have to be seen in a holistic framework, as 'part of a movement to connect more intimately with a sense of meaning in life generally'. They can be used very effectively in psychotherapy, he says (but, then, so can so many other keys to open patients up and Main says that the contents of a coincidence can, in terms of finding a meaning within it, be similar to the contents of a dream).

He includes our inability to judge probabilities as one of five possible explanations for them. The other four are: Jung's idea of a collective unconscious; a super-intelligence, for instance, God, controlling them; ESP or other psi faculties; and, finally, a scientific explanation relating to laws of the universe that we do not yet understand. He and Curtis believe that by examining the coincidences that occur to us we can find profound insights into ourselves and our lives. One thing that they are right about is the fact that the more you look for coincidences, the more you find them.

5
The Undiscovered Country

Hamlet called it 'the undiscovered country, from whose bourn no traveller returns'. Was he right in saying that no travellers come back from the realms beyond death? There are plenty of people who believe they have been able to talk to – and even see – the spirits of the dead. The survival of the human spirit beyond death is an accepted tenet of religious faith. For many people, that is enough. But there are others who need to be in touch with their friends and relatives who have died and who believe they have been in communication with them, either directly or through a medium. Is there any real evidence of an afterlife? Have we got proof?

The real answer is no: nothing that would completely satisfy the scientists and the sceptics. But we've got plenty of near-proof, plenty of examples so convincing and so inexplicable that the burden of the evidence would lead most people to say yes, human beings do survive death. How this happens, whether they survive indefinitely, what kind of existence they have after death, we really do not know. There are thousands of mediums claiming to get all sorts of messages from beyond death, a great many of whom are satisfying individual demands for reassurance: a message from Uncle Albert that he's happy and well and that Auntie Ethel should take care of her arthritis, may be enough to convince the recipient of the reality of an afterlife beyond all shadow of doubt. This is not enough to provide viable proof and there are plenty of ways that mediums, consciously or unconsciously, can cheat their clients into believing that their information comes from deceased friends and relatives (see chapter 7). Laying fraud aside, there is also always the possibility that the medium gets the information through ESP, by tuning into the mind of the recipient and picking up their thoughts about Albert and Ethel, rather than by a communication from the dead Albert.

Proof has to be subjected to much more rigorous scrutiny. Fraud has to be completely eliminated. The information conveyed has to be so detailed that ESP is ruled out (everything we know about ESP suggests that it is at best patchy and unpredictable. Nobody can tune into another person's thoughts as if tuning into a radio station and take in everything. The best that can be picked up is occasional unconnected scraps of information, as though the radio was receiving an enormous amount of interference.) Cryptomnesia, or forgotten memories, have to be eliminated. In other words, the information brought from beyond death has to be so detailed, so particular, that it could not have come from any other source and so carefully witnessed that there can be no doubt but that it came from only the dead person.

Can any evidence fulfil these tough criteria?

Well, perhaps. In recent years, the most convincing research in Britain on 'drop-in communicators' has been carried out by Dr Alan Gauld, senior lecturer in psychology at Nottingham University. Drop-in communicators are those who come uninvited and unexpected to mediums, who do not know the medium or any of those sitting with them, and who give information about themselves that can be checked and verified. They are important because their information cannot be put down to ESP: if no one present knew them, or anything about them, the medium cannot be picking up the information from the minds of those there. It is possible that cryptomnesia takes place (that the medium or one of the sitters has read an obituary or some other source of information which has been forgotten by the conscious mind but is stored in the memory and released at the seance). What makes

Alan Gauld's research special is the painstaking care he has taken to eliminate any possibility of connections between the medium, sitters and the communicator, and any possibility of cryptomnesia. En route, he also effectively eliminated fraud.

Communicators 'dropped in' to a group of people who met in Cambridge to use a ouija board during the last war on a regular basis. They continued to meet as a home circle until 1964 and had an ever-fluctuating membership apart from the couple who founded the group. Remarkably, they kept excellent records of almost every sitting: four hundred and seventy out of a total of five hundred and fifty. On the whole, they were as much concerned with producing physical phenomena as anything else and did not get too excited about their unexpected guests, although they did make a few attempts to check out the information they received.

Alan Gauld, then a student at Cambridge, joined the circle in the late 1950s, interested in the physical phenomena, which included table tilting, raps, fluorescent patches of light, the spraying of perfume and whispering noises. Coincidentally, he heard the sitters talk about the drop-in communicators who had visited them. At the time it was thought that the records had been lost. Subsequently, they came to light when the couple who initiated the sittings moved home, when they were found stored in a loft. They gave them to Gauld, who set about systematically investigating them − between thirteen and twenty years after the communications had been received. The time gap was far from being a disadvantage and actually adds to the genuineness of the case. If anyone had been deliberately fraudulent and had gone to immense time and trouble to research the stories of these unknown communicators, they would hardly have left their careful work lying around in a loft for twenty years, narrowly escaping being lost or consigned to the dustbin.

Of the two hundred and forty 'spirits' who communicated through the ouija board, the vast majority were relatives or friends of the sitters. There were thirty-eight in all who were 'drop-ins', who did not know or have any connection with anyone in the circle. Thirteen of them gave so little information that it was impossible to even begin to check out whether they had really existed. Another fifteen have not been verified: the information given does not match records. The remaining ten have been at least partially verified, some of them strikingly. In every case, Dr Gauld has gone to elaborate lengths to investigate the possibility of the medium or the sitters having access to prior information about the communicators. He has researched birth, marriage and death certificates, military records, published obituaries. He has compared details given at the sittings with descriptions and information given by surviving relatives and friends. Here are two examples:

On 3 July 1950, a seance was held at which 'Peter', a regular spirit communicator who did not give his surname, introduced 'a new member of my circle', Tommy Whitlock. Tommy spelled out the following message on the ouija board: 'Please try to contact me. Tyneside Scottish. Tall, dark, thin. Special features. Large brown eyes. Second loot. Attached Northumberland Fusiliers. Died fourteen July sixteen.'

Over the course of another ten sittings, Whitlock gave more information about himself. 'Look me up. Nottingham holds a record. I would laugh if doubted when you confirm my existence.' He said his mother was with him.

In answer to a question from one of the sitters, he said his likes were problems, Pepys reading, watercolour painting. One morning, the couple who ran the ouija board sessions felt independently that they knew the name of the road where Whitlock was born. The husband dreamt it and when he was about to tell his wife she responded with the same name before he had spoken it, Powis Street. When asked about it the next time he appeared at a sitting, Whitlock said, 'I knew it well. My association took my memory there.'

The sitters made a brief attempt to check out these facts. They assumed that 'Nottingham holds a record' referred to a war memorial, and they contacted a relative who was visiting Nottingham to check for a memorial: none was found.

When Alan Gauld took up the case, he checked the War Office official list, 'Officers died in the Great War of 1914-18', and found a 2nd Lieutenant ('second loot') T. Whitlock of the Northumberland Fusiliers, who was recorded as killed in action on 19 (not 14) July 1916. His death certificate said the fourteenth and, when Gauld checked again with the Army Records Centre, it transpired that the death certificate (and the ouija board) were right and the official publication was wrong.

Whitlock's birth certificate shows that he was born in Nottingham, a fact that is printed in an obscure book published in 1917, *Tyneside Irish Brigade* by Joseph Keating. In the book, Whitlock is listed as being in a Tyneside Irish battalion of the Northumberland Fusiliers but War Office Library records show that, at the time of his death, he was attached to a Tyneside Scottish battalion, confirming the ouija board again.

Gauld was able to confirm with relatives of the dead man that he was tall and thin with large brown eyes. At school, he won a form prize for mathematics and physics, suggesting he did enjoy 'problems'. He later enrolled for a science course at Nottingham University which was interrupted by the war. Nobody in the family could recall any specific interest in watercolour painting, but it was believed that an ancestor of theirs was a friend of Pepys. Tommy Whitlock was not born in Powis Street, but near it. (He did not say he was born there, but only that he knew it well.) 'Nottingham holds a record' could have been a reference to the war memorial at the grammar school, where Whitlock's name appears. His mother was, indeed, dead.

Having established that the information given by the ouija board was correct, Gauld had to eliminate any possibility of those at the seance knowing it by other than paranormal means. An extensive trawl of the national and local Nottingham newspapers revealed a mention of his death but this gave no date and was limited only to his name, rank and regiment in four national newspapers on 26 July 1916, as part of a list of war dead. Two local papers carried a paragraph each about him, but they listed the wrong rank (Lieutenant instead of second Lieutenant) and there was no mention anywhere in print of him being attached to the Tyneside Scottish battalion. Neither was there a description of him or a list of any likes and dislikes (although the fact that he was at the university was mentioned in the local papers and in the obscure book by Keating).

All in all, it seemed clear that there was no possible single source for all the information Tommy Whitlock gave about himself through the ouija board. Thorough checks into the background and history of all those present at the sittings has shown that none of them had any connection with Nottingham and only one of them had ever visited the city (she only went for one day and she was never one of those with her finger on the glass while the ouija board was being used).

One of the sitters was from the north-east and knew of the existence of the Tyneside Irish battalion but he had been in a different regiment during the First World War. He, too, had never operated the ouija board while Whitlock was communicating.

In the following case, the name of the communicator and addresses have been changed, to preserve the anonymity of surviving relatives.

The communicator was an angry, elderly German, who swore in English at the sitters and said he was a friend of Hitler. He said Hitler was 'the mastermind' and denounced religion as 'bloody rot'.

At subsequent sittings, he calmed down and gave some information about himself. His name, he said, was Gustav Adolf Biedebmann. He lived in London at a house called Charnwood Lodge and was over seventy when he died. He said he had his own business and 'in some remote way I am associated with the Lond(on) University'. He said he died a year before the sittings, in 1942. When he was asked if his business was publishing he replied 'Rationalist Press'.

Gauld discovered that the name Biedebmann was unknown in either German or English, but that Biedermann is a German name. In 1964 he traced a Dr Gustav Adolf Biedermann, who was a member of the British Psychological Association, and who at the time of his death (a year before the 1942 sittings) had lived at Charnwood Lodge, Bickley, Kent. Biedermann had previously lived in Muswell Hill, so it was true that he had lived in London (and the Bickley address is just outside the Greater London area). Biedermann had an interest in a sausage skin business, but he was a Rationalist and left money in his will to the Rationalist Press Association. He worked in the Psychology Department of London University.

Interestingly, Gauld was given the following assessment of Biedermann from someone who knew him: 'He had the blunt, arrogant, obstinate and aggressive manner of the typical Prussian Junker. Hence he was not well liked. But when one got past the outer façade he turned out to be quite a pleasant companion. He was, like your communicator, fond of denouncing things – and I am pretty sure one of them would have been religion.'

The information the sitters acquired could have been known to them only if they had obtained Biedermann's will and death certificate, which would have required deliberate and time-consuming fraud. There was no easy source for the information, no way in which they could have read it and forgotten it.

If these were Gauld's only cases, it would perhaps be possible to dismiss them as a fluke or be persuaded that fraud was involved. But there are others, equally good, as well as many that are confused and contain incorrect information mixed with some verifiable details. Drop-in communicators are widely reported by mediums: what makes this collection so exceptional is the degree of record-keeping that went on, coupled with the extensive research undertaken to establish not only the truth of the details given by the communicators but the lack of opportunity for the sitters to have consciously or unconsciously absorbed the information from elsewhere.

Gauld is not the only investigator to have looked so closely at drop-in communications. Other cases which throw up a similar quantity of detail have been thoroughly researched in Iceland.

The most obvious way of assessing the case for an afterlife is to look as critically at all mediumistic communication, whether it be 'drop-in' or from someone known to the medium or the sitters. It is hard to rule out the possibility of the information being obtained by ESP (but, even if this is involved, the sceptics would be forced to admit the paranormal pedigree of the information).

It is unfortunate that the most comprehensive and most critical surveys of the work of mediums are those done on the big names of the early days of psychical research: Mrs Leonard and Mrs Piper (see chapter 1). Unfortunate not because there can be any doubt that they were in the top league when it comes to mediumship, but because any investigation carried out so long ago is tainted with a suspicion that it might not have measured up to today's standards, despite the fact that early researchers were very thorough and not at all gullible. Why, say the sceptics, do we not have such astonishing examples of mediumship today?

It is possible that we do. At the turn of the century, when psychical research was a popular and respected academic pursuit, there were enough wealthy people around to give their time and money to investigating it. Today there are few who can afford to give up either, and it is not a top priority for government or philanthropic funding. Mediumship itself is out of fashion: there are famous platform mediums (the late Doris Stokes, Doris Collins, Stephen O'Brien) but their audiences are as much concerned with entertainment as communication. Plenty of mediums working privately have their own followings and scores work in Spiritualist churches but general scepticism of their abilities may be encouraging others to keep their talents to themselves or their close circles and discouraging their development. The study of mediumship is not a key part of modern parapsychology or psychical research, although many members of the SPR visit mediums as part of their quest for evidence of the supernatural. Most of them report very patchy, mixed results: the occasional snatch of uncannily correct information in a sea of irrelevance.

'I have over the years seen quite a few mediums,' said Dr Alan Gauld. 'They are on the whole rather disappointing. But there are odd, interesting things that come through. Once, I gave a medium a letter from Professor Broad, a previous President of the SPR. She gave a very accurate description of him, described his room with a writing table. Then she said that he was a bishop, but immediately changed that because, she said, he was laughing at that suggestion. She continued by saying she thought he was a bishop because he was wearing gaiters. Then she said he wasn't as *broad* as me.

'When I told Tony Cornell, who knew Broad, he said that the professor sometimes wore spats in winter. I can't explain that away in terms of telepathy, because I did not know about the spats.'

In the days when mediumship flourished, there were many physical as well as mental mediums. Mental mediums are those who claim to see or hear spirits present around them, and to communicate messages from them. The medium is usually perfectly conscious throughout, although may sometimes be in a trance-like state. Sometimes the medium writes 'automatically' words dictated by the spirits, as though they have taken over control of her arm and hand. Sometimes he or she speaks as though possessed by the spirits.

Many amateur mediums discover their gifts through working with others round a ouija board. A ouija, which takes its name from a combination of the French and German words for 'yes' (*oui* and *ja*) is a board with the letters of the alphabet, single numerals and the words 'yes' and 'no' around it, and a pointer, which can be purpose-made or improvised with an upturned glass. Usually, one or two people have their fingers on the glass, which moves around the board spelling out messages or answers to questions. (The precursor of the ouija board was a planchette board which has a pencil attached to the pointer with which spirits write or draw their messages rather than letters round the board.) The ouija was a popular parlour game during and immediately after the First World War, when many families were trying to contact relatives lost in action. Today it is condemned by fundamentalist Christians as dangerous because they believe it opens a door for evil spirits. It is more likely to be dangerous if it contributes to some already-established mental disturbance in one of the sitters.

Physical mediumship usually develops from mental mediumship. In its simplest form it involves some physical manifestation of the presence of an intelligence. Raps that can not only be heard clearly, but with which it is possible to communicate in a primitive code, for example. (Other physical phenomena, like table tilting, curtains billowing and lights swinging may be evidence of the paranormal, but they alone are not evidence of mediumship because they do not involve communication with anyone or anything else.) The most advanced physical mediums claim to be able to produce a substance called ectoplasm, a white fluid-like substance which can appear from various different parts of their bodies and which can form itself into different shapes. Sometimes it forms 'vocal chords' and enables the spirit to speak directly, in its own voice, to the sitters. This usually involves the use of a 'voice trumpet' to amplify the sounds being made and explains why trumpets are part of the standard 'kit' of the caricature medium. In very ambitious cases, it is claimed that the ectoplasm forms itself into human shapes – sometimes just a hand or a head, sometimes a whole recognizable body.

While the opportunities for fraud in physical mediumship exist, they demand more complicated skills than those used in mental mediumship (see chapter 7). The medium has to be a very adept conjurer and impersonator, and almost certainly needs accomplices if he or she attempts anything big like the full 'materialization' of human figures. Sceptics say this is why physical mediumship is practically

111

non-existent nowadays, when infra-red cameras could be used to detect fraud without upsetting the dark conditions the mediums say they need to produce ectoplasm. Mrs Helen Duncan, the last of the famous physical mediums (see page 126) was variously condemned as a heartless trickster and fraud and lauded as a rare and gifted medium who allowed photographs to be taken of her materializations. (Some early photographs exist of her producing ectoplasm, and there are photographs of other mediums from whom a white substance appears to be emanating.)

There are physical mediums operating today. In 1990, the Noah's Ark Society was established in order to bring together people interested in the development of physical mediumship (not necessarily their own). The organization now has over three hundred members, with forty-six 'circles' of seven or eight people holding seances all over the country. Members are somewhat divided as to whether the Society is Spiritualist by religion. The majority of the members have come in via Spiritualism, but there are some who feel that the emphasis within the circles should be primarily on phenomena and not involve any religious input.

The circles operate secretly in the belief that they would attract a great deal of hostile attention and accusations of fraud if they opened their doors to the public. They deny that this is because the physical phenomena they produce would not stand up to scrutiny.

'We have to be careful because it is very easy to snipe. We need to guard against being infiltrated by those who only want to make a mockery of our achievements,' said the President of the Society, Alan Crossley. A retired newsagent, Mr Crossley hosts a circle in his mobile home near Chester where, Mr Crossley claims, the medium, a businessman from Humberside, manages to get a voice trumpet to wave about in the air regularly.

'We have to protect people who have these gifts,' he said. 'The mediums can easily be damaged if they are disturbed when they are in deep trance and spirits are working through them. Because the world is so sceptical, we need to nurture them privately amongst people who will support and help them until it is time to go public. We provide a safe haven for physical mediums, so that they cannot be exploited or ridiculed.'

At a residential seminar in Leicester in May 1991, ninety-five members of the Society were present when a twenty-nine-year-old physical medium, known only as 'Lincoln' to protect his identity, from one of their circles in the south of England is claimed to have made trumpets and a tambourine wave about, messages appear on screwed up pieces of tissue paper which floated down on to the laps of the person they were intended for, and voices of 'spirit guides' to be heard. All those present were convinced they had witnessed true phenomena but they were all committed to a belief in physical mediumship in the first place.

'We advise him to remain anonymous because he is young, his talents are only just developing. If his identity was known there would be so many people beating a path to his door, it would be hell. Mediumship is a fragile thing,' said Alan Crossley. 'He has one sitting a week, with his own circle, and that's all he should do at the moment.'

The main impetus for the formation of the Noah's Ark Society was a physical medium called Rita Gould, from Leicester, who has now stopped giving sittings for members of the public. Mrs Gould was a materialization medium who had a whole repertory company of characters she could 'create' at her seances. She did not produce ectoplasm, but fully-formed beings were claimed to appear, including her grandmother, who in life was a professional singer, and would always give sitters a burst of song in a sweet soprano voice; her father, who did not talk but played the xylophone; and Helen Duncan, the medium who died in 1956. She also materialized a nine-year-old boy who gave his name as Russell Byrne and asked the sitters to contact his parents, who live in Essex. Gwen and Alf Byrne visited Mrs Gould for four or five years to be reunited with their son at seances, and they are in no doubt that it really was him.

'It was him all right. He really wanted to make his comeback and let us know he was well,' said Mrs Byrne.

'Russell was a cheeky little boy who wore me out with his chattering,' said Alan Crossley. 'I asked his mother if he was always like that in life, and she said he was. He could be really irritating. He used to run about tidying up the room. When Helen Duncan materialized I recognized her voice instantly, as I had known her in life. Her daughter attended a seance, and confirmed that it really was her mother. Helen would stand by the fireplace wearing a black dress – she always dressed in black in life. She had the same personality: forceful.

'Rita also materialized my wife for me, which was a very moving moment.'

Alan Crossley spent a week staying with Rita Gould and her husband and attended seances every day.

Professor Archie Roy also attended seances with Mrs Gould, as did three other members of the Society for Psychical Research. Unfortunately, before they were able to set up proper scientific controls and use infra-red cameras, Mrs Gould decided she was no longer going to give public sittings. The friend whose house she used for her sittings became ill and she was unhappy about continuing in other surroundings.

'Helen Duncan warned her to stop, because it was getting dangerous for her,' said Alan Crossley. 'She is not a young woman and she really did not need to risk herself. It was a great shame, because she was one of the greatest talents I have ever seen in forty years of studying physical mediums.'

Sceptics would say she got out just in time, before the cameras and the controls came into the seance room. Professor Roy is baffled by her.

'The seances were held in total darkness, and lasted for about three hours, with perhaps a ten minute break in the middle. My hand was taken a large number of times by other hands. Even in the darkness it was possible to see some things.

'When Rita Gould's grandmother materialized she sang

in a rather good voice, and she took my hand and ran it along her cheek, which was the cheek of a young woman – she materialized as a twenty-year-old. She reeked of a rather heavy perfume, which I expected would linger after she had gone, but it didn't. I don't know any way of turning perfume off. When the child Russell appeared I ran my hand down his leg, and it was the bare leg of a child. When Helen Duncan appeared she sat on the couch next to me and I felt it go down. She was a very bulky woman. I talked to her for an hour, and she had a genuine east of Scotland accent.

'At one seance, we used a torch with red paper over it, and I clearly saw the feet of the child Russell and, then, his face. It was the smiling face of a child. I saw Helen Duncan's big fat legs, the legs of a stout woman in middle age. She kept hitting me in the arm as she talked and it was the forceful hit of a strongly-built person.

'The first time I went there I was in a bit of a daze – I felt like a prospector wondering whether we had struck gold. But the final conclusion has got to be that we do not know any more than we did previously, because we failed to get the infra-red equipment in. It was a terrible disappointment. Yet if it was faked, there would have had to be a lot of people in on it, including a child. I've thought about it endlessly but, finally, I can only pass the old Scottish verdict: Not Proven.'

Professor Roy is happier with – though no less cautious about – the proof of an afterlife offered by the recent Antonia case of hypnotic regression in America. Hypnotic regression involves getting subjects, under hypnosis, to re-live 'past lives'. It has been practised for over a hundred years, but in the last thirty-five years has become much more popular (as has hypnotherapy generally). *The Search for Bridey Murphy*, a book about an American woman's past life as an Irish peasant girl, triggered much of the interest, but experts have since criticized this case for not taking account of the amount of knowledge about life in nineteenth-century Ireland that the woman could have acquired through normal means. Similarly, several interesting cases recorded by Cardiff psychiatrist and hypnotherapist Arnall Bloxham have been criticized. Even those who believe that the past lives of some subjects are genuine admit that, under hypnosis, many people are capable of fantasy that far outstrips their waking imaginative ability. The Antonia case has confounded many of the critics, however, and although Professor Roy is not prepared to commit himself to the case being proof of survival and reincarnation, he says, 'I am forced to the conclusion that the details of this case could not have been given in any normal way. If we get more cases like this it will be very difficult to avoid accepting that the past is in some way in existence today. Whatever else, this is a very good case for paranormal activity.'

The Antonia case is the story of an American woman, Laurel Dillman, who was regressed by a group of amateur hypnotists, and believes that she once existed in the sixteenth-century as a Spanish girl called Antonia. The personality of Antonia, once awoken, seemed to take over Laurel's life and she eventually sought help from a professional hypnotherapist, Dr Linda Terrazzi. Dr Terrazzi listened to the story of Antonia as it surfaced when Laurel was under hypnosis. The story itself is the classic material for a romantic novel. Young Antonia was born in 1555 on the island of Hispaniola, brought up there and in Germany, went to England with a German uncle after the death of her mother and took part in the plot to replace Queen Elizabeth I with Mary Queen of Scots. After the failure of the plot, she fled the country to join her father in the town of Cuenca in Spain. On arrival she found that her father had died and took over his ailing inn and paid off his debts. She was imprisoned by the Inquisition and raped by one of the Inquisitors, with whom she subsequently fell in love. She became his mistress, bore him a son and travelled with him around the world before drowning off the coast of Peru.

Dr Terrazzi, convinced that it was nothing more than fantasy, decided that it would help Laurel if she could

ABOVE The Edinburgh team. Professor Robert Morris (foreground), who has the Koestler Chair in Parapsychology at Edinburgh University, and members of the team working with him. From left to right: Deborah Delanoy, Robin Taylor, Helen Simms, Richard Wiseman (academic and part-time magician), Don McCarthy, Caroline Wall and Charles Honorton, the American whose ganzfield work is recognized as one of the most significant developments in parapsychology.

RIGHT Dr Sue Blackmore, a believer-turned-sceptic.

LEFT Tony Cornell (left) and Howard Wilkinson with SPIDER, their electronic device for monitoring poltergeist activity.

RIGHT Archie Roy, Professor of Astronomy at Glasgow University and an expert on the paranormal.

BELOW Dr David Fontana (right) with the Matthews family in their haunted workshop. From left, Pat Matthews, her brother Fred Cook and John Matthews.

ABOVE Ghostbuster Maurice Grosse, with a computer printout of temperature changes in haunted premises.

RIGHT Rev. Anthony Duncan, a Church of England exorcist.

BELOW Dr Serena Roney-Dougal, who is exploring theories linking ancient beliefs with the latest scientific research into how the brain functions.

ABOVE Alan Crossley, founder member of the Noah's Ark Society which aims to foster physical mediumship.

RIGHT A traditional Spiritualist: Mrs Jean Bassett of the Spiritualists' National Union.

BELOW Two women who believe that Spiritualism and Christianity are not mutually exclusive: Mrs Iris Ingarfill (left) and Mrs Beattie Scott.

ABOVE Michael Roll, retired Bristol estate agent, dedicated to establishing the existence of the spirit world by scientific means.

LEFT The unbelievers: Toby Howard (left) and Dr Steve Donnelly, editors of *The Skeptic* magazine.

prove this to her: so she set about researching the story. During forty-five sessions spread over a seven-year period she recorded several hundred facts, including the names of residents of Cuenca, the address of a college that Antonia attended, and obscure details of the banned index of books in different provinces of Spain.

Obviously, some facts were well-known and hardly required checking: the plot to overthrow Elizabeth I, the building of the Spanish Armada and so on. Other facts could be researched in libraries of a reasonable size. But there were some facts that could only be found in rare books at specialized research libraries and more were not published in English at all. The most difficult category were those that were not in published form at all, but which existed in local archives, written in old Spanish.

Dr Terrazzi enlisted the aid of seven American professors of Spanish history, who were intrigued by the detailed questionnaire she sent to them. Over three years, and after a visit to Spain to research Inquisition records, Dr Terrazzi found that every single fact given by 'Antonia' was true. Names and addresses of her friends and neighbours in Cuenca, names of the inquisitors, even oblique details like the fact that the Inquisitor who raped her said that the sentences he gave citizens caught in acts of fornication had been considerably moderated since he had been involved in such an act himself which was borne out by the records of punishments meted out by the Cuenca inquisition. To fake the story, Laurel Dillman would have had to spend years researching the story of Antonia. No book has been found that contains all, or even a substantial part, of the detailed information she gave about life in sixteenth-century Spain. The professors who collaborated with the research are agreed that it would be a long-term scholarly project to assemble all the facts. Dr Terrazzi has examined many different possible explanations apart from reincarnation, including cryptomnesia (forgotten memories) and possession. Ultimately, she has concluded that the only one that tallies with all the facts is the reincarnation theory – and that's what Laurel Dillman herself believes.

In looking at cases of hypnotic regression, Professor Roy believes there are seven important criteria:

1 The life recalled should include a large number of details.
2 The details should be capable of verification (if they cannot be verified they need not necessarily be untrue, but they have no value as evidence).
3 When checked, a high proportion of the details should be true.
4 A high proportion should be so difficult to verify that a long period of research into a wide variety of sources is necessary.
5 A good proportion of the sources should be outside the education and experience of the subject.
6 The life of the subject should be investigated to make sure that it was not possible for them to have carried out the necessary research.
7 An independent assessor should look at both the subject and the investigator to eliminate any possibility of fraud or collusion.

Professor Roy believes the Antonia case goes a long way towards meeting all these criteria.

Reincarnation cases are more common in countries whose culture supports belief in it. The most thoroughly-researched cases have come from non-Christian countries and have been investigated by Professor Ian Stevenson from the University of Virginia. Professor Stevenson is the world authority on reincarnation cases and has investigated over two thousand in more than thirty years of research. He believes that historical hypnotic regression cases are more susceptible to fraud, cryptomnesia and fantasy, and prefers to work with spontaneous childhood memories of previous lives. He has a caseload of studies with young children who can give details about previous lives which are recent enough to be checked thoroughly.

Working with young children offers many advantages: they have not had the chance to assimilate information from other sources; they have no appreciation of a fraud motive (although their families may have); their shorter lives are easier to investigate. The wealth of verifiable detail is the answer to critics who say that young children fantasize: they do, but their fantasies do not provide factual evidence of another person's life, often with very little overlapping their own. Young children would require a lot of coaching for the family to perpetrate a fraud.

Stevenson investigated a case in the Lebanon and, by the time he arrived on the scene, the child was five years old. Apparently, the boy's first word had been 'Jamileh', and as soon as he could string words together he told of his previous life as Ibrahim Bouhamzy (Jamileh, it transpired, was Ibrahim's mistress), who lived in a village twenty miles away, in an area of the country where roads were poor and, traditionally, people did not move far from their own villages.

The boy, Imad Elawar, was told off by his parents for telling lies but persisted with his story. They did nothing to investigate the facts, so when Stevenson arrived he was able to interview Imad at great length and visit the family of Ibrahim Bouhamzy to check everything out. Fifty-one out of a total of fifty-seven statements were correct. When the two families eventually met, the Bouhamzys were amazed that the five-year-old child behaved so like the old man who had died. Here's a brief summary of some of the details the young child had given:

He named Bouhamzy, but did not give the first name, Ibrahim. He named the mistress, Jamileh, and said that she was beautiful and wore high heels (unusual among the Islamic Druse sect). He said that Bouhamzy had a brother, Amin. In fact, Amin was a close relative and these are sometimes loosely termed brothers. The boy said Amin worked at Tripoli, in a courthouse, which was correct.

He named Bouhamzy's sister correctly and gave the names of two brothers, who were, in fact, cousins. He named a friend of Bouhamzy's and gave details of a road accident that one of Bouhamzy's close relatives had been involved in. He described how Bouhamzy was fond of hunting, gave details of his guns and where one (illegal) gun was hidden. He described his house correctly, noting that there were two wells, one full and one empty. He gave a description of his dog and remembered Bouhamzy beating off another dog. He described a car, a minibus and a truck belonging to Bouhamzy, he knew where the tools for the car were kept and, although he was wrong in saying that Bouhamzy had two garages, the vehicles were kept in front of two sheds.

He was right about Bouhamzy's livestock – goat and sheep – but completely wrong in saying that he had five sons: he had none. One of the cousins that Imad named had five sons.

The massive weight of detail rules out coincidence and Stevenson's extensive research rules out collusion.

In another case, in which an Indian girl claimed a previous incarnation as a married woman in a town a hundred miles away, extensive efforts were made to check on the girl's duplicity. The girl first talked about her previous life when she was three and could still remember it in great detail when she was ten. When members of her other 'family' visited her, they tried to mislead her by assuming the wrong identities: she was able to see through this. Again, there is a vast weight of detail about her previous, unexceptional life. Perhaps it is the ordinariness of Stevenson's cases, compared with the romantic-novel glamour of most hypnotic regression, that lends them authenticity.

Stevenson, like Dr Alan Gauld, is reluctant to commit himself on what his research proves. He goes so far as to say that it suggests an afterlife is a possibility. Gauld, who is Britain's foremost expert on life after death, says:

'Somehow we make a mark on the universe which survives our demise and may be picked up by others. There are lots of possibilities.'

He says that we will only know for sure after a great deal more time-consuming and painstaking work.

'By the time this work has been even partly carried out, most of us will be dead and will thus know the answers anyway, or not know them as the case may be,' he says in his book, *Mediumship and Survival*.

An outline of the sort of work that is still needed was given by Professor Bob Morris to the annual conference of the SPR in 1991.

'We could be doing a lot more to organize our data and to find out what information we should be looking for when we carry out investigations. For instance, we can have several different models for how we survive death:

- People who survive bodily death are able to contact us, they are organized and they are eager to be in touch. This has been asserted very often in mediumistic communications and in different philosophies. We need to know its variations and themes, its consistencies and inconsistencies across cultures.

- They are disorganized and communication is difficult, awkward, there is a strain of sorts; the world is not like it used to be. We could try to establish what kind of difficulties, what kind of distortions. We could do more research on the kind of characteristics that might make someone a more powerful communicator, circumstances that might enhance or increase the ability to communicate.

- There is also the unquiet death. When someone has died with unfinished business some aspect of them sticks close to the earth for a while still trying to complete it. This is an idea present in many different cultural and social systems. What are the themes? What kinds of deaths, what kinds of lives did they have. Where can we look for further examples?

- Place memories. Not a case where there is any semblance of intelligence or direction, but the idea that some places seem to be able to recycle information that happened there: the lady in white holding the candle comes down the staircase and goes out through the wall, and does that every time, does not smile, does not chat, simply replays the scene. What kind of circumstances are conducive to this kind of happening?

'We are writing about all these things, but what we need to do is explore each case much more fully, look at the social and cultural diversity, set each case within the context of one or more of these models.

'There may, of course, be models that are a little harder to get at, in which survival is not seen as an intact functioning entity; or the idea that a distinct self may pass on to other realms but does not communicate further. And, finally, perhaps we should think about the aspect of self that is capable of survival, capable of propagation of information.'

Professor Morris believes that by working out the kind of information needed and by standardizing the questions asked and the reports written about cases of survival to some extent, it will be possible to analyse them and come up with much clearer ideas of the form that survival takes.

This is for the future. In the meantime, the distinguished psychologist and psychic researcher Robert Thouless, who died in 1984 aged ninety, left behind a puzzle that could instantly solve the question of proof for survival of bodily death. He encoded a message, and promised that after his death he would come back and decode it. To date, although one or two mediums have claimed to be in contact with him, none of them have come up with the solution. They say that he is working hard at trying to remember it.

Religion

At the beginning of this century, half the population of America was Spiritualist. In Britain, the Spiritualist movement, though not as strong, was very well-established. A whole religion had sprung up around the paranormal. The belief that it was possible to communicate with the spirits of the dead had launched not just a wave of serious scientific research but a new faith. There were some who rejected their old religion – the vast majority of converts to Spiritualism were Christians – and there were others who tried to reconcile the two.

Spiritualism has a claim to a history stretching back to pre-Christian times, when ancestor worship was acceptable and talking to the spirits of the dead was routine. Its emergence as a religion in its own right came in 1848, when the Fox sisters (see chapter 1) were discovered. Prior to them, most communication with spirits had been at a rather elevated level: the biblical prophets talked with God, Joan of Arc was guided by the voices of saints and angels. Maggie and Katie Fox were getting messages from a very ordinary man who told them his name was Charles Rosna and that he had been murdered and buried under the house where they were living. (Investigations confirmed some of his story and bone and teeth samples were found in the cellar.) Despite the tragedy of his death, Rosna had no claim to fame or exceptional immortality. His ability to communicate from beyond death offered the first proof that ordinary mortals could not only achieve the eternal life offered by Christianity but were within reach of the living. The dead did not have to have anything particularly religious or even wise to say in order to communicate with the living. Anyone could be contacted, consulted, kept as part of the family. It was inordinately comforting for those who had been bereaved.

Controversy still surrounds the mediumship of the Fox sisters. But while they were variously lauded and criticized, the world adopted the movement they had begun.

It was exciting. Mediums were discovered all over the place and their seances were wildly diverting: tables levitated, trumpets waved through the air, 'apports', or gifts, were brought from the dead. It beat stuffy old church three times on Sundays into a cocked hat and swept America. By 1855, Spiritualism had two million followers in the States and was catching on in England. It spread more slowly in Britain, probably because the established Church of England had a greater hold. None the less, it won some distinguished converts, including Sir Arthur Conan Doyle, the creator of Sherlock Holmes, Robert Owen, a leading Socialist and one of the founders of the Co-operative movement, and Sir William Crookes, a prominent physicist. When the Society for Psychical Research was founded, with a highly-respected academic membership, thirteen of the original seventeen council members were Spiritualists (although this proportion decreased rapidly).

Spiritualism was attractive because apart from the great fascination of the phenomena – messages from the dead, levitations and so on – it offered ordinary people a chance to practise their religion within their own homes, without pomp and ceremony, without a priesthood who were set apart from the congregation. It was a small, intimate religion, cosy, essentially comforting and cheap to run.

Towards the end of the last century, however, the boom was over. Many fraudulent mediums had jumped on to the bandwagon and had either cheated so blatantly that nobody was fooled or been exposed by psychic investigators. Their behaviour brought the whole movement into disrepute and led to all mediums being tarred with the same brush. The intelligentsia who had originally been so enthusiastic now backed off. Society ladies who had enjoyed table-tilting sessions at their tea parties became bored. Spiritualism retreated into the homes of small dedicated groups. It was no longer a middle- and upper-class preoccupation but became entrenched in the working classes.

The departure from the mainstream religions' centralization of power that had been one of Spiritualism's original attractions soon developed into a freedom that was to precipitate its undoing. At first, anyone could claim mediumship and shamelessly exploit those who desperately sought to contact their dead relatives and friends. It became necessary for Spiritualism to become more structured. There were attempts to form larger groups, many of which foundered almost immediately. Without funds, without traditional administrative skills and with so many ordinary people who found themselves unexpectedly in positions of leadership that they were unwilling to relinquish, factions and disputes were inevitable. There was a genuine fear that a large national organization would attract people who were more interested in the office than in the religion.

Eventually, two national (now international) organizations emerged: the Spiritualist Association of Great Britain and the Spiritualists' National Union. By the turn of the century, they were legally constituted bodies, although Spiritualism was not recognized as a religion with legal status until 1951. Today there are about one thousand two hundred Spiritualist churches in Britain, with an estimated eighty to one hundred thousand people worshipping in them regularly. *Psychic News*, the Spiritualist newspaper, was established by its first editor, a well-known medium called Maurice Barbanell, in 1932, and one Spiritualist magazine, *Two Worlds*, dates back to 1887.

The public's cynicism about Spiritualism, which was fostered by another rash of blatantly fraudulent mediums who set up to exploit the desperation of the women whose husbands, sons and sweethearts were lost in the First World War, led the Spiritualists to feel that they were persecuted during the years up to 1951, when the last Witchcraft Act was repealed. It is a difficult issue: the law believed it had a duty to protect innocent people from exploitation, particularly at a time when they were so vulnerable. There were plenty of unscrupulous so-called mediums around and prosecuting them was no different from any other consumer protection. There were clients who went to mediums and came away feeling they had been ripped off, both financially and emotionally. Set against this, there were others who went to the same mediums who were convinced that they had genuinely been in touch with the spirits of the dead.

The question of payment was central to the arguments for and against prosecution. If a medium based in a Spiritualist church was working for nothing more than her expenses, she could not be accused of exploitation. If, on the other hand, she was charging commercial rates and making a good living out of it, then she had to be seen to be giving value for money: a very subjective judgment where mediums are concerned.

Certainly, prosecution seemed a terrible waste of the country's time and resources when, in the closing stages of the Second World War, the Central Criminal Court at the Old Bailey was occupied for seven days with the trial of the famous medium Mrs Helen Duncan. Mrs Duncan was accused under the Witchcraft Act, along with others who had arranged her seances. One of the alleged offences was that they 'exercised or used a kind of conjuration that through the agency of Helen Duncan spirits of deceased persons should appear to be present in such place as Helen Duncan was then in, and the said spirits were communicating with living persons there present'.

The prosecution paraded witnesses, some of whom felt they had been conned out of the 12s 6d (about £15 today) that they paid, while others were convinced that they had met their loved ones. Helen Duncan's fame rested on the fact that she was a physical medium, who claimed to be able to conjure up the actual physical forms of the spirits she was in touch with. Her opponents alleged that she impersonated these 'spirits' herself and that the ectoplasm she seemed to produce was in fact cheesecloth or muslin which she swallowed and regurgitated to order.

The Prime Minister, Winston Churchill, expressed his irritation that one of the most important courts of the land should be taken over by such a case. For some observers, though, it provided light relief against the backdrop of the war. The Spiritualist movement considered the case was far from trivial. The sentencing of Helen Duncan to nine months' imprisonment seemed like a savage blow against them. However, the public backlash against this case was to lead to the repeal of the Witchcraft Act and the institution of the Fraudulent Mediums Act, and see Spiritualism established as a recognized religion.

Helen Duncan was a renegade within the movement. She had been approved by the Spiritualists' National Union but, when she started holding seances again after her release from prison, they decided that her powers had waned and withdrew their diploma, saying that her seances lacked adequate control. Her problems with the law were not over. In 1956, a seance she was holding in Nottingham was raided by the police. Five weeks later, she died and her supporters maintain that her death was brought about by the shock and injuries she suffered from being disturbed while in a deep trance. She was substantially overweight (she weighed twenty-two stones) and in bad health anyway, but it is probable that the shock accelerated her death, whether she was fraudulent or genuine.

The Helen Duncan trial was the last major milestone in the acceptance of Spiritualism. The law today takes a *laisser-faire* attitude towards mediums, leaving people free to choose whether they want to pay to visit them. While there are undoubtedly many fraudulent mediums still exploiting the gullible and vulnerable (see chapter 7) there are far more who are genuine: whether or not they have mediumistic powers is open to doubt, but their intentions and their belief in their own abilities are unquestionable. Because of its nonconformist roots and the autonomy of so many of its churches, the Spiritualist religion encompasses a variety of different beliefs. For instance, about half of all Spiritualists believe in reincarnation, while the others do not. Some churches have hymn singing and prayers, imitating the style of worship in traditional churches which many members find they miss when they convert to Spiritualism; other churches keep their meetings more informal (although they must all adhere to one legal requirement if they are to be accepted as a religion, which is that they must have public services incorporating some reverence to a deity).

The widest division with the modern Spiritualist church is between those who accept Christianity and those who do not. Most Spiritualists do *not* believe that the road to salvation and life everlasting is through an intermediary, Jesus Christ, whose blood can atone for their sins. They have no sacred book and no single leader. They accept that Christ existed, as also did Buddha and Mohammed, and argue that they were teachers not divinities.

The Greater World Christian Spiritualist Association,

however, represents a hundred and fifty affiliated churches where traditional Christian beliefs are practised alongside Spiritualism, without the approval of the established Church of England or the Roman Catholic Church. The Greater World beliefs are based on the teachings of a spirit guide called Zodiac who, in the 1920s, communicated through a young woman called Winifred Moyes, explaining that he had been one of Christ's teachers in the temple at Jerusalem and that the Christian and Spiritualist messages were one and the same thing. Although they do not accept the doctrine of blood atonement, they believe that God and the Great Spirit, as worshipped by other Spiritualists, are the same thing, and that Christ is the accessible bridge to God.

President of the Greater World Association, Mrs Iris Ingarfill, believes that other Spiritualists have 'thrown out the baby with the bath water' by rejecting Christian teaching. Despite their fundamental differences, the Greater World maintains a good relationship with the other Spiritualist organizations.

Mainstream Spiritualist beliefs are the same throughout the non-Christian part of the movement: man is in eternal progression, one stage of which is to appear on earth in a physical body in order to learn lessons that can only be learnt through contact with physical matter. Man is essentially a spiritual being, but at this stage in his development he is fettered by a physical body, which limits him. Inside, he is a perfect replica of his physical, outer case so that, when he progresses beyond death, he sheds the case but retains the form and attributes that are individual to him. His spirit 'body' is filled with light and colour (some mediums claim to be able to see 'auras' around people, which correspond with these colours emanating from the spirit). Charles Coulston, general secretary of the Spiritualists' National Union, likens our time on earth to a 'term at boarding school. We board in the physical world for a short time only. Death is like the beginning of the school holidays because we go back to our real home in spirit.'

The afterlife is not a geographical place, but a different state of being. It interpenetrates our own world without us being able to detect it unless we are mediums. Even they are only able to tune in to the frequency of the next stage of development. According to these beliefs, there are many levels that we can aspire to. On the next, closest frequency, we retain many of our human characteristics. It is a comforting, if flippant, thought that after death according to the Spiritualists we will still be able to make love, enjoy a drink, smoke, walk the dog. We will be wearing our normal clothes and will look the same, except that we will have shed our physical defects. Even more seductive is the promise of being reunited with the friends and family we love. Eventually, as we evolve into more spiritual beings, there will be no need to perpetuate these very earthly pleasures and relationships; but in order to aid our transition they will, at first, all be there for us.

Spiritualists believe in a perfect god, the Great Spirit, of whom we are all imperfect copies. They use readings from the Bible in their services, although not specifically Christian ones, and they have their own words for traditional hymn tunes. They depart from recognizable church services with their demonstrations of clairvoyance, which almost always follow the short act of worship. A medium will take the stage and bring 'messages' to members of the audience. The standard of presentation varies enormously: some mediums are in great demand and travel all over the country at the expense of the churches, others are very local and familiar to the audience. Most mediums are women.

'I don't believe that is because women are born with more potential than men, I believe it is because women are more sensitive to their own abilities,' said Charles Coulston. 'Many men are so busy earning a living that they don't have time to develop their mediumistic talents and the pressures of their lives often drown out their abilities. Some discover their potential in later life, when they have more time on their hands.'

Most churches run 'developing circles', where members

are shown how to make the most of their talents as mediums.

Unlike most other religions, only a small proportion of Spiritualists are born into the faith. Most discover it for themselves, the majority probably after a bereavement. Many do not share their faith with other members of their family.

'There are plenty of outsiders who have a strange idea of what being a Spiritualist is like,' said Charles Coulston. 'They see us sitting around in darkened rooms, calling "Is there anybody there?" and watching the table tilt.'

Spiritualists are able rather tortuously to reconcile their beliefs with Darwin's theory of evolution by involving their teachings about the souls of animals. Apparently, animals only have group souls and are absorbed into 'group spirits' when they die. However, if a pet is loved as an individual it acquires an individual soul and for at least the first part of its life in the spirit world remains with those who loved it on earth, before eventually being absorbed into the group spirit of its species. At the primitive, apeman stage of Darwin's evolutionary ladder, human beings had only group souls, too: their spiritual evolution has kept pace with their physical evolution.

Poltergeists and hauntings are accommodated within Spiritualist teachings as earthbound spirits who can be helped on to the plane where they should be existing by a sympathetic medium. A good medium can 'read the history of a building from its walls, listen to it like putting a needle on to a record' says Mr Coulston, but he stresses that these are very minor activities for mediums. Some apparitions are, he says, reactivated thought forms, others are the spirits trying to show themselves in human form (for instance, when someone clearly sees their dead spouse or relative sitting on the edge of their bed). Crisis visions are caused by the spirit body sending out a signal at the time of death. If the death was violent or sudden it may be difficult to completely get rid of the physical form, and this may also give rise to apparitions.

The essence of Spiritualism is belief in survival in

a very recognizable and essentially human form after death, not in the nebulous and indeterminate afterlife offered by the mainstream religions. Within the context of Spiritualism, all paranormal phenomena are acceptable and explicable.

Christianity and the Paranormal

There are many fundamentalist Christians for whom spirits are real, visible (if not tangible) entities. They may not accept the teachings of Spiritualism, but their concept of an afterlife is based almost as closely on a physical re-creation of this world in which spirits inhabit recognizably human forms and are concerned with many of the same problems that preoccupied them on earth. The Bible contains many references to phenomena that today would be considered paranormal: spirits, angels, visions, apparitions, seers, miracles, speaking in tongues. There are Christians whose religious beliefs are based on a literal, not symbolic, interpretation of the Bible. For them, the existence of ghosts, poltergeists and other manifestations of the paranormal can easily be encompassed by their religion.

Every diocese of the Church of England has a 'deliverance team': ministers who have chosen, alongside their normal parish duties, to help when problems of 'unquiet spirits' are brought to them. Although, today, the victims of poltergeists and hauntings might go to psychic researchers for help, a good number still turn automatically towards the church which for centuries offered the only help and counselling available in these cases. The deliverance team can exorcise the troubled spirits that are causing the problems.

'It is my belief that when the majority of people die they set out immediately on their journey to God. But there are a few – for the most part those who die very suddenly or violently – who somehow don't seem able to go to their rest. That's why we call them the unquiet dead,' said Canon Dominic Walker, a qualified psychologist and co-chairman of the Christian Delivery Study Group, and a leading member of the Church of England's deliverance team. The deliverance team can call upon support from trained counsellors, doctors and psychologists, as well as priests.

The Church's Fellowship for Psychical and Spiritual Studies is less concerned with fieldwork and more interested in monitoring the academic work being done in parapsychology and mainstream psychical research. The Fellowship has its own journal, *The Christian Parapsychologist*, which carries articles about the relationship of the paranormal to the Church's teachings and reviews selections from the huge amount of literature on the paranormal.

The Fellowship was established in 1953 by Col. Reginald Lester, a retired army officer and journalist, and a number of his friends. It was founded because the Christian Churches, by and large, looked askance at any involvement in the psychic realm and thought it impossible to be involved with people who were psychically sensitive without being caught up in Spiritualism.

'In the early days, there was, in fact, a strong spiritualistic element in the Fellowship, but we have been at pains more recently to make it a Fellowship in which psychic sensitivity is explored within an orthodox Christian milieu,' said the Venerable Michael Perry, Archdeacon of Durham University and chairman of the Fellowship.

Most of the members are Anglican lay people but there are priests and ministers from the Anglican, Roman Catholic and Free churches in the Fellowship.

'In any group of people, a certain number will be found to be naturally psychic. These "sensitives" have an intuitive attunement both with their fellows and with levels of reality that transcend the rational capacity of the mind,' says a leaflet of introduction to the Fellowship. 'Such levels may include spontaneous glimpses into the past and the future, awareness of the disposition of other people and, at times, even communication with those who are physically dead.

'This, not unnaturally, causes unease to those who do not understand these matters, but these qualities are not necessarily damaging and, indeed, ought to be beneficial if used in the environment of the Church . . . Some people are more sensitive than others, and if their sensitivity is dedicated to God they may be particularly valuable in the fields of healing and counselling, including counselling the bereaved . . . The Fellowship has become more and more an arm of the Church as its particular expertise has helped those in the ministry of deliverance as well as those in more usual healing and counselling work.'

In the field, ministering deliverance, away from the committees and the journals, are the priests who are called out whenever paranormal activity is reported. Canon Anthony Duncan, who has been involved in the ministry of deliverance for over twenty years, does not see himself as a psychic researcher. Although, when bringing help, he tries coincidentally to get to the root of the problems he sees and sometimes finds he must try to understand the phenomena.

Canon Duncan's own psychic gifts are hereditary. His mother was psychic and his paternal grandmother was a gifted medium. He is of highland Scottish extraction and, among the highland Scots, there is a strong tradition of second sight.

'I think I had always known I had some psychic abilities, but it was not until I was serving in my first parish in Gloucestershire that my psychic senses woke up with a bang and I was pitchforked into this ministry, when we found we were living in a haunted vicarage,' said Canon Duncan, who now has a parish in Northumberland and who is a member of the Study Group.

'I discovered all kinds of sensitivities that I did not know I had. There had been disturbances before, but all of a sudden it seemed to erupt when we were there. We discovered we were sharing the place with not just one but two former incumbents. It all cleared up within three months.

'I was lucky enough to be able to call on the help of Dom Robert Petit Pierre, who is no longer alive but was one of the greatest church experts on psychic matters, and also another priest who was just down the road who had plenty of experience. The whole church and churchyard had to be cleaned up psychically, by exorcism.

'After that, my newly-won experience was in demand. I was also Chaplain to the Bishop of Oxford in these matters and I have been a consultant ever since – I hate the word exorcist because it has too many connotations attached to it by Hollywood movie-makers. I've been busy ever since, although you can have periods of up to six months when nothing happens, suddenly, then, you will be rushed off your feet. In this diocese, there are three of us priests doing the work, and I'm the senior one. Sometimes we work together, sometimes we just consult each other. But I believe more and more clergy are becoming aware of the importance of this ministry and, very often, all I have to do is give advice.

'I don't think it helps to be psychic. You can perform this ministry just as well if you are not, as long as you are not sceptical and dismissive about the evidence being presented by the unfortunate people who are able to see, hear and feel things that you cannot. But because I am psychic I can use my own antennae when I go to a situation, I can sense what is happening, even if I don't immediately understand it. I'm not excessively sensitive. In normal life, I don't go round having strange feelings and insights about people and situations. But it seems that when I am faced with someone in need something switches my sensitivities on.'

Canon Duncan was recently called to a house in a nearby parish where the residents were alarmed because strange and unexplained noises had been heard, objects had moved around when people were out of the room and the children living there, although unable to articulate it, seemed always to be upset.

'I could tell straight away that there was a demonic, evil spirit in the house. Sometimes hauntings are just some lingering unhappy memories, sometimes there is an unhappy, earthbound spirit, a previous resident. But when there is something demonic it is always the result of some human misconduct, because as the New Testament tells us Satan was cast out and he only gets his toe back in if we specifically invite him. The misconduct can go back generations and it may lie dormant. Perhaps it just has its time for coming out, maybe there is some trigger.

'Things are usually quite bad by the time I get called in. The people living there are often rather reduced, physically and psychologically. The cause of the trouble is usually in the place, not a person – in twenty years I have only seen three genuine cases of humans being possessed. But the place may be possessed because of the evil brought in by a previous inhabitant, or because of dabbling in witchcraft or magic. Once you know what you are dealing with the church tells you what to do, and you just fire at it with both barrels. You invoke the saving victory of Christ against the evil one, and you feel the mischief clear away immediately. You know in your heart if your diagnosis is right.

'As far as exorcism goes, it is always done under the authority of the Bishop: no priest just does it off his own bat. I always take another priest with me, to provide covering fire. Sometimes it takes two or three goes – there may be more than one problem to deal with. It is highly stressful and exhausting, potentially lethal. The battle with the evil one has to be fought somewhere, and it is fought in one's own self. You feel the pressure, you feel the battle and you feel as though you are going to burst. I've heard of priests dropping down dead in the middle of exorcisms. I suspect they were not doing it right, but even if they were the pressure could certainly precipitate a heart attack. Sometimes you can almost see the force you are battling with. After an exorcism, I arrive home completely drained.'

Canon Duncan, who was born in 1930, recently exorcised a pub in Northumberland, after a heavy keg of beer was thrown across the cellar at the publican. He was called in by the local vicar, who was not sensitive to psychic feelings, but admitted that parts of the pub had a chilling effect on him. The pub, which had been converted from a row of cottages, had been partially rebuilt. It was in the old parts that there was a feeling of menace and particularly in the cellar.

'I could see the hole that the beer keg had knocked into the wall. Just showing us down there made the publican white and shaky, he nearly passed out. I laid hands on him and put him back together, then left him and his wife saying the Lord's Prayer while we went back into the cellar. After we'd finished, the room seemed even to change shape, it was so different.

'We went back upstairs and said confession for somebody, I don't know who. Perhaps there had been a murder committed there at some time.'

But exorcism is a drastic treatment, and Canon Duncan reckons he can sort out most problems rather less dramatically.

'It is far more common to be dealing with an unhappy earthbound soul. Somehow you have to get through to it – it's not very different from dealing with anybody else. You establish a rapport. I usually say "Don't you think we ought to say our prayers, dear?", then help them make confession, absolve them and commit them into the care of the holy angels. That's about it. Except that you often get this extraordinary sensation of the whole house heaving a sigh of relief.

'It's really rather simple. The only thing that isn't, is the diagnosis. But over twenty years it becomes easier to detect what's going on. Some inner voice tells you what it is about, and you get told that Heaven is involved. You also have the general corpus of experience and knowledge that the Church has built up.'

Canon Duncan is not sure whether the received wisdom – that poltergeists depend on the energies of a disturbed person who is present – is correct. He feels that although the problems often do stem from a confused adolescent, they can equally well come from a mature person or a person who is no longer living, explaining the poltergeist cases where there does not appear to be any single focus.

'It is rarely one simple diagnosis. I was called to one house where there had been classic poltergeist activity, stretching back over a number of years. The wife was very sensitive and was near to the point of a breakdown. I exorcised the place. It was the spirit of a chap who had hanged himself there and I was able to send him on his way. A fortnight later, I was called back because there was a series of tappings and bumpings coming from the ceiling: this time I found that it was the wife causing them. I think she missed being the focus of attention and so her energies were being used to cause more disturbances. After I blessed her everything settled down peacefully.

'At another house I went to in Gloucestershire, they were having problems keeping a housekeeper. They had pulled down a lean-to kitchen and built on an extension that was the housekeeper's accommodation but three or four women had given in their notice after only being in the job a matter of weeks. The last one who left said she could not "be doing with all these goings on". She said she had seen a rug move across the floor and it "gave me a proper turn". Whenever she took a tray down it was replaced on the shelf as soon as her back was turned. She described it as being chased around her own kitchen.

'I am not often clairvoyant – I usually feel presences rather than see them. But when I went into the kitchen I clearly saw this furiously aggressive little cook, who had died about the turn of the century, but did not seem to realize she was dead. She was living in the kitchen as it was in her time, and the new people with their new kitchen were impinging on her and making her angry. I told her I was a priest, and that it was my duty to tell her she was dead and should not be there. She said she wanted absolution. I started to say the Church of England liturgy, but without any prompting I found myself putting in extra bits. I realized I was using the words of the Roman Catholic service: she was an Irish Roman Catholic.

'There was another presence in the same house. The nursery had been made out of part of the landing, which was large. But despite being cheerfully decorated it was a grey room and there was a smell, like the smell of death, in there. I realized there was a man standing by the window, looking out. He had been looking out for years before he died, across the meadow towards the town. I realized that he had convinced himself that he had done something that could never be forgiven, and yet I could feel that he was a good man. When I'm dealing with spirits, I know things about them without them actually speaking to me. It took me a long time to get a rapport with him, but when I did I told him the Lord likes sinners and he eventually agreed to move on. As he went, his depression lifted from the room and it became sunny and happy.

'I don't actually hear the confession they make, but this was the only occasion in twenty years when I knew what it was. As I was giving him absolution, the lady who owned the house came in to tell me she had put the kettle on. As she walked in I heard her make a strangled noise and run out. I did not stop: I was busy . But afterwards over a cup of tea she told me that when she entered the room she felt a couple of hands go round her neck and start to strangle her. I said, "That's what he confessed to me he had done". Yet until she said it, I had no idea what he had told me. You see, it's not me he's confessing to, it's God. I'm just the vehicle. It's irrelevant whether I know what he says or not.'

Sometimes the residents do not mind the ghosts or spirits that haunt their buildings. Several years ago, Canon Duncan was called to the British Legion club in Tewkesbury, because a relief steward had been upset one night after closing time to see a monk walk from the billiard room and disappear through a wall. Canon Duncan persuaded the monk to move on.

'When the regular steward returned he said he could have told us about the monk because he was a frequent visitor. He said he would miss him now he was gone.'

He knows of families who co-exist happily with their ghosts, often giving it a name. One friend of his has an old man who sits in the corner smoking strong-smelling tobacco: he does not bother anyone, so the family are happy to let him stay.

'Perhaps he's just visiting to have a look at his old home,' said Canon Duncan. 'It is only when the spirit is causing trouble that it is definitely earthbound. I don't get called in when there is no trouble. After all, you don't send for the doctor when you are healthy.'

Although he gets called out to council houses, Canon Duncan is not surprised that old buildings yield the most hauntings: more people have passed through them, so more unquiet spirits have been left behind. Vicarages and rectories are also popular with ghosts.

'In years gone by they could be very tormented places. The vicar had to lead a life of perfect rectitude, put on a good public face whatever happened. Vicarages were also places where the general public directed a lot of tensions. And they were perfect targets for the devil. If I was Satan I would direct my power at the vicarage. Why waste powder and shot? Go to where it can do the maximum damage.'

Canon Duncan does not know why some spirits remain earthbound. He suspects it is because at the time of their death they were particularly inward-looking, obsessed with their own problems and interests. Although many have met with violent ends – as though death came so suddenly that they were unprepared for it and not ready to leave earth – he has equally encountered some who have died after lingering illnesses, which should have given them plenty of time to prepare. He also knows that only a small minority of those who are murdered or die in untimely accidents do not seem to be able to make the transition to the next world.

'There don't seem to be any rules about who will stick around, adrift, hanging on to their earthly existence.'

Although his work brings him into contact with the spirits of the dead, he is not happy about attempts to contact the spirit world initiated from this side.

'I think when spirits hang around, they need help. But, although I'm not dogmatic about it, I don't think we should be attempting to call them up at will. Anyone who has a faith knows there is an afterlife. They don't need to talk to their dead relatives and friends in order to prove it. I don't accept the idea of heaven as a continuation of life on earth, although being with God, which is what heaven is about, begins right here on earth.

'I accept other phenomena that some people would call

paranormal. I became aware of the reality of telepathy ages ago. My wife Helga and I have a tremendous telepathic rapport on a rather trivial level. We know what the other is thinking, quite unprompted. I would never try to do it – that would be like eavesdropping, rather impolite. We have always kept dogs and cats and anyone who is familiar with animals knows that telepathy exists. With one of my dogs I only had to think the word 'walk' and he would be by the door. Children are naturally telepathic, but as they get older they learn to conform and block it out.

'I don't believe you can test for telepathy in laboratories – thank goodness. If it could be harnessed it would end up being used for military purposes.'

He believes that he has been called by God to minister to those having problems with unquiet spirits – and to minister to the spirits.

'My ministry is about people, I don't differentiate between those who are living and those who are dead. It happens to be what I am good at. Some priests are good at working with youth. I'm hopeless with youth, but I'm OK with spooks.'

6

Quantum Leap

Hang on to your hats, you're in for a bumpy ride. You need a background of high-level physics or maths to understand what's going on at the frontiers of science. It is difficult for the rest of us to take on board the implications, let alone the theory, of the 'new' physics. But it is essential if we want to make sense of the supernatural.

Psychic events and paranormal experiences are rejected by many people – possibly the majority – because they do not fit in with our accepted framework of reference. They break what we think of as the laws of the universe. Telepathy, for instance, is regarded as an impossibility because there can be no link between people miles apart unless it is by telephone, radiowaves and so on (in other words, a man-made or man-manipulated link). There is no easy explanation for the fact that two people appear to be able to communicate with each other without these aids, telepathically. So it is dismissed as a figment of imagination, wish-fulfilment, or as chance coincidence, the chance greatly increased if the two people concerned are close to each other and likely to share similar interests and thought patterns.

Perhaps, instead of looking for ways in which to make psychic experiences conform to our 'laws of the universe', we should take a good look at those laws and ask whether they should be changed instead.

This is exactly what physicists have been doing for the whole of the twentieth century. Of course, the impetus to reassess the laws did not come about as a by-product of trying to explain the paranormal: most physicists would still, even today, run a mile from any suggestion that the new discoveries made in their world have got anything to do with ghoulies, ghosties, long-leggety beasties and things that go bump in the night. No, the pure physics and mathematics came first, with the splitting of the atom and Einstein's Theory of Relativity. It is only now, as we begin to grapple with the implications of such major discoveries, that we can see that the anomalies of the paranormal may not be anomalies at all, but perfectly explicable within the framework of the new understanding we have of the world in which we live.

Or, more correctly, the new understanding that the scientists and mathematicians have. The vast majority of the population haven't a clue what is going on in these specialized fields. We don't need to understand the mind-boggling implications of the new physics, because they don't impinge upon our everyday life. We know that there are nuclear weapons and most of us are concerned about them. We know there is such a thing as nuclear power. We may know that a lot of industries use radioactive processes. We may even know that lasers and transistors, with all their multiple uses, are a by-product of sub-atomic physics. But that is likely to be the limit of our knowledge: few of us have a concept of the enormous scientific breakthrough that gave us these things.

We are living through the most exciting developments in mankind's understanding of the universe since Galileo told a credulous world that the sun was not revolving round the earth. Galileo was forced to retract his teachings by the angry Roman Catholic Church which needed to see the earth as the centre of God's creation. We have not forced our modern-day quantum physicists to retract and abandon their work, but by failing to take on board the profound implications of their discoveries we are relegating them to the obscurity of science textbooks.

Many people do want to understand what is going on. Stephen Hawking's book, *A Brief History of Time*, was on the bestseller lists for a record number of weeks. Still, most people who bought it and tried to read it found it impenetrable and consigned it to the bookcase or the coffee table. It was a bit like giving a child *Bleak House* as its first reading book. In physics terms, most of us are still at the Janet and John level.

We've taken the word 'quantum' into everyday usage and we talk about a 'quantum leap' as a major spring forward in reasoning and thinking. But very few of us have seriously attempted the quantum leap of trying to understand this very term.

It *is* very difficult. We have been brought up in the mechanistic world of Newtonian physics. It does not matter if you never studied physics at school and the only thing you know about Isaac Newton is that an apple falling on his head helped him formulate his theory of gravity – you are still living your life according to Newton's laws, and you still have a basic instinctive grasp of many of the principles of Newtonian physics.

Newton brilliantly drew up the mathematical formulae to explain the world as people knew it three hundred years ago and still know it today. It is Newtonian physics that tells us that if we push the salt cellar across the table to the person opposite too hard, it will end up in their lap and that if we don't push it hard enough it will stop before it reaches them. Newton worked it all out mathematically and, given the right information, he could have calculated exactly where the salt cellar would come to rest. Without any detailed knowledge of physics or maths, we all have a basic understanding of this.

It was Newton who explained gravity mathematically but, from the beginning of civilization, men have understood that if they drop something, it will hit the ground and that if they up-end the salt cellar, salt will come out.

Newton, in other words, made scientific sense of what we already knew. He was also able to extend that to things we didn't know, mathematically predicting the existence of the planet Neptune before astronomers had found it. When it was found, however, it was actual and real and visible.

Newton's genius is readily recognizable because his physics deals with the world as we see it all the time.

When today's physicists – of no less genius – come along and start telling us about things we cannot see, things that cannot be easily recognized in the everyday world around us, we react with indifference. The scientific world may have been excited for almost a century by sub-atomic physics, but the rest of us are happy to leave them to it. After all, we can be told that the salt cellar we push across the table is made up of masses and masses of vibrating molecules and atoms, all of which can be split into sub-atomic particles which rush around creating and destroying other particles, but this knowledge doesn't make the salt come out any quicker or alter the way the cellar hits the floor when it's dropped. It does not, as Newton's laws do, explain anything that we already know instinctively or anything we need to know about the salt cellar.

It requires an imaginative leap to think of a solid object as really a seething mass of atoms, so it's not surprising that the information that sub-atomic particles don't behave in any of the ways scientists would expect them to is far beyond our grasp. They completely overturn the laws of Newtonian physics. So what? We cannot understand the relevance of these discoveries until we take on board the massive theories about our universe that follow on from them, theories so vast that they sound like farfetched romantic nonsense and they require such a revolutionary way of looking at and understanding the world around us that most of us never make the starting gate. These theories, and the scientific facts on which they are based, will certainly be accepted by generations to come, who will look back on our Newtonian view of the mechanical universe with as much amusement as we regard the flat-earthers.

What follows is an attempt to present, in the simplest possible terms, part of the story of twentieth-century physics and to look at some of the theories that have been extrapolated from the scientists' findings. Among these theories, perhaps we will find some explanations for what we now call the paranormal, phenomena which may in future be scientifically accepted as nothing more nor less than normal.

The New Physics

It was not Newton's fault. He knew the limitations of his work. He described himself as 'a little boy playing on the seashore and diverting myself in now and then finding a smoother pebble or a prettier shell than ordinary, while the great ocean of truth lay all undiscovered about me'.

Those who came after him treated his work as though it was the whole ocean of truth. Newton's physics was so clear and complete – and so effective – that by the end of the nineteenth century young science students were being advised by their university professors to go into chemistry and biology because there was little or nothing left to explain in physics. The universe was a huge machine which functioned according to verifiable mathematical laws.

Philosophers had a problem with this: the idea that human life in all its complexity was nothing more than a by-product of some highly sophisticated mechanics was to them a denial of the existence of the soul, of individuality and even of God. They wrestled with the enormity of these issues, while the scientists went on discovering more and more evidence which conformed to Newton's laws.

By the beginning of this century, scientists were beginning to discover the limitations of Newtonian physics. Newton was not wrong: his laws still apply very adequately in the physical world we all recognize. Beyond this recognizable world, however, within the minutiae of sub-atomics, there is a great deal that cannot be explained or predicted by Newton's physics. And at the other end of the scale, in the vast world of space, Einstein's theories have overtaken Newton's. Einstein's theories assault our common-sense appreciation of the universe just as much as the study of sub-atomic particles does.

The discoveries made by Einstein and the sub-atomic physicists have made science more challenging and have also introduced to it all the mystery and mysticism of a religion. Physicists discussing quantum theory are as likely to be locked in debate over 'free will' and 'consciousness' as they are over the scientific concepts of bifurcation and entropy.

The scientists may be able to take the theory and the mathematics involved in quantum physics on board rather better than the rest of us but they are just as bemused by its implications. Einstein himself tried very hard to frame all the new discoveries into the old, classical physics, because he too felt threatened by something so new and so vast.

'All my attempts to adapt the theoretical foundation of physics to the (new) knowledge failed completely. It was as if the ground had been pulled out from under one, with no firm foundation anywhere upon which one could have built,' he said in his autobiography.

It was Einstein who overturned two of the basic laws of Newton's safe, mechanical universe. Newton believed that space was immovable and that 'absolute true and mathematical time, of itself and by its own nature, flows uniformly without regard to anything external'. Einstein proved that space was, in fact, curved, and that time was relative to the speed of light – the hands on a clock travelling at the speed of light will stand still because at that speed time does not move. If individual observers travelled at different speeds they would have different perceptions of time and each one would place events in a different order. The speeds involved, of course, would have to be unimaginably greater than anything we experience in our daily lives. Technically, a clock speeding from London to Edinburgh on an Intercity 125 records time differently from a clock sitting stationary on a mantelpiece but the difference involved at these low speeds would be infinitesimal.

Einstein demonstrated that space and time are the same thing and make up a fourth dimension for the universe: spacetime. We cannot visualize a four-dimensional world – even Einstein and the brightest of the physicists who have come after him could not comprehend four dimensions in anything other than the language of mathematics. Modern scientists have had to go beyond the Newtonian idea that in order to understand something we have to have a picture of it in our heads. Throughout the new physics we are dealing with ideas that can only be expressed mathematically: we don't have any other language to frame them in.

If we accept that there *are* four dimensions – length, breadth, width and duration – then we are in a static universe, with no past, present or future. It is our own consciousness that brings in the idea of time, the idea of our lives moving inexorably forward from birth until death. It is our illusion of the universe that things happen in sequence, that we are moving through time and the illusion is caused by our movement through the universe (just as when we travel in a train we get the illusion that the trees and hedges and telegraph poles are rushing forward).

The most famous of Einstein's theories is the universally-recognized formula $E = mc^2$, which expressed his discovery that energy has mass and mass has energy. In the formula E = energy, m = mass and c = the speed of light. The energy contained in even the tiniest piece of matter is equal to its mass multiplied by the speed of light squared so that each piece of matter gives off enormous energy (the speed of light is a phenomenal 186,000 miles per second). Mass and energy are therefore different forms of the same thing. But the destruction of mass (which releases its energy) only takes place at the heart of stars, in nuclear reactors and in atom bombs. The development of the bomb, whose existence has overshadowed the twentieth century, was an unforeseen and unwelcome development of pure scientific theory.

We are already into some heavy, incomprehensible stuff and we have not even started on quantum theory yet. Quantum mechanics is, in essence, the study of sub-atomic particles. Since the time of the ancient Greeks, it was assumed that the atom was the smallest unit into which matter could be split. Newton accepted that atoms were the building blocks of the universe and his theory of gravity explained why these tiny lumps of matter would bind together to make the solid objects we see all around us. He described them as minute but very dense.

Early in this century, it was discovered that atoms themselves were not dense and could be divided into particles. As the smallest thing we can see under a microscope contains millions of atoms, and as the particles inside each atom are very much smaller still (if an atom could be blown up to the size of a fourteen storey building, its nucleus would be the size of a grain of salt in the middle, with a few dust particles revolving round it) we are dealing with a world of unimaginable minuteness.

We are also dealing with particles that are nothing like dust specks. A speck of dust is a real, tangible object; it belongs to our safe Newtonian world. A sub-atomic particle cannot be seen as an object – although in some experiments it may behave like one. Scientists found that although these particles sometimes collide with each other and cannonball off as if they were tiny lumps of matter (i.e. particles), at other times they behave like waves, spreading out and dissipating without any solid core. Nor do they follow a predictable trajectory around the nucleus – one minute they are here, the next minute they are there. These are some of the fundamental anomalies of quantum mechanics. How can an electron or any other sub-atomic particle be both a particle and a wave? Why is there no sensible pattern to its motion?

Time and time again, experiments have shown that we cannot measure both the position and the velocity of a sub-atomic particle but only one or the other, another mind-boggling fact that sits uneasily next to our notion of a comprehensible world in which all things are definable. (A car, for example, can be measured for both mass and speed, as the manufacturers are at pains to illustrate every time they try to sell us a new model.) Sub-atomic particles can only be measured approximately – the more precisely mass is measured, the less we know about speed and vice versa.

What's more, scientists can work out probable patterns of behaviour for particles in general, but they can never say how one individual particle will behave. Our knowledge of sub-atomic particles can be compared to our knowledge of the life patterns of all female babies born this year. Statistically, it is true that they will have a life expectancy of seventy-five years, will marry when they are twenty-three and will have 1.8 children. Of course, we would not expect these figures to tell us anything about the future life of an individual baby. In the same way, we can make statistical predictions for sub-atomic particles, but there's nothing to say any individual particle will conform to them. Scientists can, in fact, make excellent predictions which can be relied upon as heavily as we rely on our knowledge of how objects behave in the concrete world about us, but none the less we have to accept that they are only predictions. We can say with great precision how long it will take for half of a piece of radioactive material to decay – but we have no idea how long it takes for any individual atom of the material to decay. Again, this is another fundamentally incomprehensible idea to those of us rooted in a Newtonian culture.

Even more radically, scientists have demonstrated that it is impossible to look at anything objectively. Einstein started it, by proving that time was relative to the position of the observer who was measuring it. Einstein, as the scientists say, put the observer back into the system. In the pursuit of a pure and disciplined mathematics, he inadvertently zoomed into the rather mystical concept that we create our own reality, that everything depends on how and from where we see it.

The behaviour of sub-atomic particles is affected by the way in which they are observed or experimented with: they do not function independently. The way in which we look at them determines whether they are waves or particles, whether they will follow one route or another. What are they doing before we observe them and make measurements of them? They may not be doing anything, but be held in a sort of limbo. Then, they are just as likely to be doing *at the same time* all the options that are open to them. The scientific theory that describes this is known, appropriately, as the Uncertainty Principle.

The best example of how this works (or doesn't work) is Schrodinger's cat, named after Erwin Schrodinger, one of the most famous of quantum physicists. Whether Schrodinger ever possessed a cat is not recorded. He probably did not, because no cat lover would ever have dreamed up this imaginary experiment, even as a theoretical exercise:

A cat is placed inside a box. The box also contains a cyanide gas capsule which, if released, will kill the cat. Whether or not the gas is released is determined by the radioactive decay of an atom, which can react in one of two ways only one of which will release the cyanide. The box is sealed, the experiment starts. A split second later, the gas has either been released or it has not. Is the cat dead or alive?

According to classical physics, all we have to do is open the box and see – the cat's fate is already sealed. According to quantum theory, though, the fate of the cat depends upon our observation of the sub-atomic particle, so until we open the box and look at the experiment, the cat's life hangs in the balance. It is neither dead nor alive until we look – or it is both dead and alive, the particle having behaved in both possible ways.

It is reassuring to know that this experiment could not be carried out with a real cat, or any other highly-complex living organism, because there are far too many other factors involved. In theory, as a thought problem only, scientists continue to face the dilemma of the cat's fate.

This is one of many dilemmas. Nothing more completely demonstrates the truth of the old axiom 'the more you know the more you realize how little you know' than a study of quantum physics.

Having originally thought there were only three types of sub-atomic particle, we now know there are over one hundred, and probably many more. We know that these particles are themselves probably composite: they are made up of quarks. Goodness knows what we'll find when we get into the realms of sub-sub-atomic particles.

We know that some particles have anti-particles, a sort of negative mirror image of them. Whenever positive and negative meet, they annihilate each other and quite literally disappear in a flash of light (photons being the particles that make up light).

We know that the decay of a particle can result in two particles spinning off from it in opposite directions. However far they separate, each carries an imprint of the other and each knows what is happening to the other, so that, for instance, if one is blocked, the other will also be blocked. Even though they may be a long way from each other, they appear to be able to communicate instantaneously with each other. And, like all other particles, their behaviour is affected by observation and so, correspondingly, is the behaviour of their matched particle, however far it may be from the observer. If one particle is spinning clockwise, the other must be spinning anticlockwise, even if they have travelled light years apart. We know by only measuring one of them which way the other is spinning.

Einstein, who was deeply troubled by quantum mechanics (his famous quotation, 'God does not play dice', reflected his feeling that there had to be some physical order in the sub-atomic world), teamed up with two other physicists, Podolsky and Rosen, in order to come up with the EPR paradox, which set out to illustrate the absurdity of quantum thought, and which postulated that the direction of spin of the non-measured particle was determined at the very beginning, when it split from its counterpart.

The EPR paradox temporarily slowed down the progress of quantum mechanics but, eventually, a Scottish physicist called John Bell came up with an experimental test for the paradox. For some years, it seemed as though this could only be a theoretical test because we did not have the technology to make it practical. Today, however, we do and can prove that particles have no spin until they are measured, but that as soon as one is measured the direction of spin of the other is known. We can force one particle to spin in a certain direction after the split: the other will still be found spinning in the opposite way. Finally, it may sound absurd but we know that particles are really nowhere until they are observed.

All in all, what the new physics has given us is a series

of paradoxes and anomalies, questions without answers, events that have no causes. Everything that we previously understood about the universe has been thrown over, all our mechanistic concepts are obsolete.

This alone is enough to make us realize that there are more things in heaven and earth than are dreamt of in our philosophies. Without formulating any precise theories to accommodate the paranormal, it becomes probable that we should accept that these comparatively minor manifestations are well within the scope of a universe that we obviously understand so imperfectly.

The word 'supernatural' is defined in the dictionary as 'outside the ordinary operation of cause and effect'. Quantum physics has demonstrated that it is possible for events to be causeless and that everything we have previously regarded as 'ordinary' is open to question.

Some eminent physicists have gone so far as to say that not only can modern physics embrace the possibility of psi but that, had it not been known to exist, physics could have predicted it. Many theories have been developed accommodating psi within the new physics and the foundation stones for even more have been laid.

The most overwhelming new concept, one that would seem to open the door to any number of different interpretations, is the idea that we have an effect on what we observe. If sub-atomic particles only decide how to behave when we decide to observe them, we are in some way controlling them. Since the universe (including the brain) is made up of sub-atomic particles, perhaps by our will we are controlling everything. The physical world can no longer be thought of as existing in its own right. It is fundamentally linked to the psychical world of the observer. Our consciousness becomes a major factor in the framework of the world we live in: a very difficult and mystical idea for Western brains, but one that seems to tie in easily with many Eastern philosophies.

The links between Eastern mysticism and modern physics have been fully explored in books like *The Tao of Physics* by Fritjof Capra and *The Dancing Wu Li Masters* by Gary Zukav. Capra finds, without forcing his argument, a substantial parallel between the mystical philosophies of Buddhism, Hinduism, Tao and Zen and the strange new concepts of the new physics. It is ironic that Newton's heirs should be the ones to overturn his mechanistic culture and align themselves with the mystical ideas that were allowed to flourish in the East but which Newton's world view suppressed so effectively in the West.

The new physics, in other words, is not so radically shocking to Eastern minds. It is an extension and scientific verification of their existing philosophies about the importance of consciousness and the observer within the system.

Einstein revolutionized the way we look at time and introduced the concept of the static, four-dimensional universe. Only our position within this universe gives us the impression that our lives move in an orderly way from a beginning to an end. If we accept this revolutionary new way of looking at time, according to some psi believers, we should also be able to accommodate the time irregularities that are often part of paranormal experiences: apparitions from another age; regression; precognition.

The non-existence of time at the speed of light does, in theory, make immortality possible. Divine beings may be those who can travel at speeds which today seem phenomenal to us, but which may not seem so odd to future generations. Einstein held that the speed of light was the one absolute we could work with. Quantum physics in some ways appears to challenge that and who is to say that, in two or three hundred years' time, Einstein's physics won't be as obsolete as Newton's?

The ability of one sub-atomic particle to carry an imprint of another, no matter how far apart they are, may eventually be found to have some bearing on telepathy and other psychical phenomena. The particles seem to be able to interact at a speed greater than that of light, which contradicts Einstein's belief that it is impossible for any communication to travel faster than light.

The human brain is able to register quantum activity: a photon of light, which is a sub-atomic particle, can be registered by the optic nerve. At any one time, there are ten million neurons in our brains which are reacting to quantum activity, that indeterminate, unpredictable activity that characterizes sub-atomic behaviour. When we are relaxed or asleep, even more neurons are susceptible to stimulation by quantum phenomena. We do not yet know how this affects our brains, but it is possible that it provides a route for thought or information transfer. One theory, put forward by physicist Evan Harris Walker, is that sub-atomic particles have a form of consciousness of their own. He also argues that because the brain involves a considerable number of random quantum processes our own observing consciousness affects brain function just as scientists affect the behaviour of sub-atomic particles in experiments. This could explain not only telepathy, but also psychic healing and psychokinesis, because consciousness could influence the quantum behaviour of distant objects or another person's body.

The 'many worlds' theory of quantum mechanics opens up immense possibilities. If, every time a sub-atomic particle is offered a choice, it behaves in all the ways available to it, the observer must split into different but identical people, each observing his chosen state of the particle in different and divergent parallel worlds. We are, in other words, constantly surrounded by (but unable to see) many parallel worlds, the number increasing constantly, for every physical interaction in this known world.

This is so farfetched a notion – and so impossible to prove or disprove – that it has not been taken seriously by many physicists. But nor has it been entirely discounted, and there are those who believe that when one world 'leaks' into another we get psi experiences such as apparitions. Linked to this is the theory that the universe is like a vast holograph of which we are all splinters and whose collective unconscious we all share. If a holograph is split into two it becomes two complete holographs of the same thing, with marginally less detail than in the original. The more it is split, the more fuzzy the detail becomes, until eventually you are left with just a vague shape.

Some physicists, most notably David Bohm, believe that the universe is not an assembly of physical objects, but a complicated web of relations between various parts of one whole. 'Ultimately the universe has to be understood as a single undivided whole, in which analysis into separately and independently existent parts has no fundamental status,' he wrote in his book *Wholeness and the Implicate Order*.

If we are, as he suggests, parts of a whole and, on the holographic principle, carry a memory pattern of the whole, then we all share a great deal of information at a subconscious level (however fuzzy and lacking in detail it may be). This is the collective unconsciousness and similarities between folklore, legends and superstitions held across the world by widely differing cultures may provide evidence for its existence. There are certain common themes that recur in all languages, all religions, all traditional storytelling. They could, perhaps, be the products of this collective unconsciousness.

An extension of this theory is that our thoughts are connected with those of others, that we are in fact connected with everything else in the universe, because we, like everything else, are composed of the fundamental particles that make up the universe (and, as quantum theory has shown, these particles can be forever linked to each other). This theory embraces telepathy, healing, psychokinesis, dowsing, you name it.

'Morphogenetic fields' is another similar theory. That's a mouthful of a name for the theory propounded by the biologist Robert Sheldrake who suggests that everything in the universe, whether a human being or a lump of rock, has a collective memory. Because of this we can learn things that have been learnt by many previous generations much more quickly than we can learn something new (which may explain why the new physics so mind boggling!).

According to Sheldrake, all living organisms and inorganic substances are organized into 'fields' which shape the development and behaviour of the group or species. 'There are characteristic organizing fields for molecules, plants and animals of every kind and also fields for animal and human behaviour. Thus a giraffe today is linked to its ancestors over millions of years not just by genetic inheritance but by previously unrecognized non-material influences. It is as if nature has a memory for the shape of things – be they animals, molecules or behaviour.'

As evidence, he cites many examples of seemingly acquired patterns of behaviour. During the Second World War, milk bottles were withdrawn in Holland but, as soon as they were reintroduced, blue tits started to open their tops just as they had done before the war. Blue tits lead short lives, and there had been a gap of several generations over the war years. Blue tits also travel in a very limited area, so Sheldrake argues that the morphogenetic theory is one possible explanation for the spread of the habit so rapidly.

As far as inorganic matter goes, Sheldrake cites the fact that new compounds are notoriously difficult to crystallize, yet the more they are crystallized the easier the whole process becomes. (If Sheldrake's morphogenetic theory is discounted, scientists offer few other explanations for why this is so.)

One important advantage of Sheldrake's theory is that it is possible to test it, at least in part. Experiments with rats in a maze shows that the more rats that work their way through it, the faster succeeding rats manage it. When English-speaking people, with no knowledge of Japanese, were given three Japanese rhymes to learn, one a traditional one well known in Japan, one a brand new rhyme and one made up of nonsense words, they all found it much easier to learn the traditional one. Similarly, when subjects with no knowledge of Persian were asked to look at Persian words, memorize them and then copy them down from memory, they scored much better with real words than with those written back to front. They scored even better when a recording gave them the correct pronunciation and meaning of the word at the same time.

Another experiment was carried out by an undergraduate in the Department of Psychology at Nottingham University. Monica England tested volunteers doing four crosswords, two of which had already been published in the *London Evening Standard* and two of which were published at a later date. According to Sheldrake's theory, the published ones should have been easier to do, having already been tackled by thousands of the newspaper's readers. The results were not clear cut: the volunteers who were given the paper's 'Easy Puzzle' did significantly better on the version that had already been published. But those given the 'Quick Crossword', which consists of single word clues, did roughly the same on both published and unpublished versions. There will, no doubt, be more experiments set up to test Sheldrake's theory in future. The testibility of Sheldrake's theory makes it one of the most attractive areas of research into paranormal means of communication, which means that work is bound to continue in this area. If convincing proof is found, it will be a major step forward for the parapsychologists.

The discoveries of the new physics have been seized upon by those who are anxious to prove survival of bodily death in scientifically credible terms (see chapter 4). A vociferous retired estate agent from Bristol, Michael Roll, has waged a one-man campaign to encourage public appreciation of the possibilities, although, like many zealots, he has been side-tracked by his obsession with a conspiracy theory, which he maintains is 'keeping these exciting new breakthroughs from the people'.

The truth is simpler: the concepts only touched on in this chapter are so vast and incomprehensible to our common sense that the law of supply and demand keeps them away from normal everyday information channels. We demand digestible bite-size chunks of information and major breakthroughs in physics do not meet these demands. Gradually, as more and more books tackle the new physics in lay person's terms, as television programmes come up with pop versions and the school curriculum is amended to introduce the ideas in the basic and simplified form suitable even for young pupils, it will begin to be absorbed.

The new physics offers a host of possibilities for explaining the paranormal. It takes to the forefront of scientific theory what has previously been deemed the realms of cranks and mystics. Even without understanding the physics, it is possible to understand that science and psi are moving closer together: if we do not understand psi, it could be because we do not yet understand quantum mechanics. With the best brains in the world addressing the quantum problem, we may not be too far from the day when everyone accepts, without question and with full scientific backing, the existence of psychic phenomena.

The Dualism Debate

There are those who believe that whatever science throws up in the future and however mystical physics becomes we will never explain the paranormal in physical terms. These are the dualists, the people who believe that human beings are not just highly-evolved monkeys with super-duper computers for brains, but that we are all essentially unique – not only in the model of our 'hardware' or the 'software' input it receives through upbringing, education and experience, but in much more fundamental terms. We have, they believe, minds as well as brains and, although the two obviously interact, they are independent of each other.

It is difficult to believe in any kind of afterlife without being a dualist. After all, if the body (and the brain inside it) are cremated, what is there left to survive if you do not believe in some integral part of the human personality which it is not possible to explain in physical terms?

The idea that man's personality was nothing more than a series of brain reactions followed naturally on from Darwin's comparatively recent theories about evolution (it is less than a century and a half since the established ideas about man's unique relationship with his Creator were overturned by the realization that we were, after all, only another point to plot on the evolutionary graph). This all fitted in with the hard materialist (Newtonian) views of the physical world which held sway at the time.

Pioneering work on the understanding of the brain seemed to point in the same direction. Brain lesions were found to impair mental functions and alter personality, which suggested that all mental processes derived from the physical workings of the brain. In the early years of this century, Pavlov, a Russian physiologist, produced some interesting work on conditioned reflexes (everyone knows how Pavlov's dogs soon learned to ring the bell and be rewarded with food) which led on to 'behaviourism', the study of how we all behave in similarly conditioned – albeit far more complex – ways. Behaviourism was the dominant force in psychology right up until the early 1960s. If all human activities could be reduced to behaviourism, there would be no need for us to have minds at all. But very few professionals working in psychiatry, psychology or neurophysiology (the study of the workings of the brain and the nervous system) believe there is no such thing as a mind. They believe it is a part of the brain, but not the controlling part.

The dualists argue that it is separate and that it is in control: as if the brain were a computer and the mind a computer operator. They believe there are intuitive and qualitative aspects to life that can never be absorbed by a scientific physical explanation, even though they accept that brain science is in its infancy.

One of the leading proponents of the dualism theory is Dr John Beloff, who is an honorary fellow of Edinburgh University, where he lectured for many years before his retirement.

'Mind and matter are, as I see it, two different things. It doesn't surprise me that the mind can sometimes do things that a computer could not – the sort of things we describe as paranormal. I don't think a physical explanation is possible for most phenomena. Quantum mechanics may offer a few alluring analogues but, ultimately, I don't believe it is a sustainable explanation.'

The quantum theory that puts an observer in any equation as a *sine qua non* is most alluring as a psi explanation: the observer is thought to be a psi source, which not only determines the outcome (as in the case of Schrodinger's cat or the spinning particles) but which can also influence it. In applying this to PK or ESP tests, Beloff argues that it would mean that the subject who scores above chance would do so because he observed that he had done so but, at the same time, he could only observe because the events had already taken place. He would be, Beloff says, like a dog chasing its own tail.

Unlike some dualists and the 'idealists' who believe that everything in the universe is a structure of mind, Beloff believes that there is a reality and that the mind reacts with it.

'I don't believe science will ever explain it all. Life can really only make sense with a dualist philosophy,' he says.

The arguments both for and against dualism are abstruse and recondite. Obviously, religious belief influences attitudes towards dualism (although it is not an essential factor: Dr Beloff is an agnostic). Without quantum mechanics, belief in the paranormal would go hand in hand with dualist belief. Since the 'new' physics, however, the ranks of those who accept psi are split down the middle.

The Third Eye

The human brain is a relatively uncharted domain. It is such an immensely complex organ that, so far, all our attempts to explore its territory have been like day excursions into the foothills of the Himalayas. The millions upon millions of cells that make up the brain function electrically and chemically to control all our body processes. Most basically, this tells us that messages from our brains allow us to wriggle our toes, tap typewriter keys, open our mouths. At a more complex level, the brain also controls the manufacture of hormones which control our growth, our metabolism, our ageing, our moods, our emotions

– everything that happens to us physically emanates from the brain.

Compared to other sciences, the neurochemical study of the brain is in its infancy. Nevertheless, we have, in the past few decades, made strides in plotting the geography of the foothills of brain activity, at least, and experts are beginning to assemble the information that will eventually lead to full-scale detailed maps.

It is a complex and difficult discipline, but it is obvious that if psi exists, if we are capable of experiencing telepathy, precognition, out-of-body experiences, crisis visions and all the other manifestations of the paranormal, then the brain must be responsible for this ability, enabling us to record and register it.

How it does this is still a matter of speculation but there is a growing body of opinion that the pineal gland, a tiny pine-shaped gland in the centre of the brain, is the seat of this ability. For many years, it was thought to be a vestigial organ, like the appendix, something that was once necessary to our functioning but for which, now we are more highly developed, we no longer have a use. Recent research has found that, not only is the pineal very much hard at work for us, but it controls some essential functions and could be the gateway to fascinating psychic abilities.

Ancient folklore talks about a 'third eye', 'second sight', a 'sixth sense'; Eastern philosophy has always accommodated the ability to communicate without using normal physical powers. The ancient yogic *chakra* belief denotes seven *chakras*, or important centres, in the body, which by meditation and study can be brought more fully to life, opening the student up to a fuller spiritual, psychological and psychic life.

The *ajna chakra* is believed to be the one that, according to yoga teacher Swami Satyananda Saraswati, 'is the receptor and sender of the subtle vibrations which carry thoughts and psychic phenomena throughout the cosmos'. Where is this *chakra* sited? In the pineal gland in the brain. Although the ancient teachers who pioneered the *chakra* system might be surprised to discover that modern science now backs up their beliefs.

Dr Serena Roney Dougal, whose book *Where Science and Magic Meet* contains a lot of detailed information about pineal gland research, stumbled on the subject by chance when she was starting her work on a parapsychology PhD more than ten years ago.

She travelled to America to give a lecture and, although she had been paid expenses to cover her travelling costs, she had no money for accommodation. So, arriving a day early, she asked some students at the university in St. Louis if they knew of anyone who would let her sleep on their floor for the night. She was offered a bed by a hospitable young couple and, that evening, discovered that her host was doing research into psychotropic plants – plants that induce altered states in the brain. He had recently returned from South America where he had been staying with a tribe in the Amazon, monitoring their use of a vine which they brewed into a drink and which caused them to have vivid hallucinations.

The same plant, known by a variety of different names, is used by many different tribes across several South American countries. The hallucinations it produces are not just for pleasure: the tribesmen use them traditionally to obtain information about their enemies, to tell if visitors are coming, to find out if wives have been unfaithful: in other words, for clairvoyance and divination.

What interested Dr Roney Dougal – and has sustained her interest through more than a decade of research – is that the active hallucinogenic chemical obtained from the vine is almost identical to a chemical produced naturally in the pineal gland. The chemical, a compound called a beta-carboline, would, if taken orally, be a very potent hallucinogen and may be responsible for altering our state of consciousness and making us receptive to psi (it is one of many natural hallucinogens found in the brain).

Beta-carbolines may also work as tranquillizers. They seem to work in a similar way to Valium, although, of course, since they are produced naturally in the brain they are non-addictive. Some of them also seem to work as natural painkillers. They are known to affect the transport of nervous impulses and they appear to be involved in controlling the body's temperature – in animals this is used to promote moulting and hibernation and other seasonal activities like mating. Research has shown that many human beings are also affected by the seasonal rhythm, having more energy in the light summer months and being lethargic and depressed in the winter.

Beta-carbolines also affect the concentrations of vaso-pressin in the blood. The hormone vasopressin is not fully understood but we know that it is secreted from the pituitary gland and is instrumental in keeping the fluid levels of the body in balance. It is linked with the condition of people who suffer from fluid retention and who put on weight even though they do not overeat.

'Vasopressin is linked with psi abilities in certain psychics,' says Dr Roney Dougal. 'It is well known that a large number of mediums and psychics have this sort of metabolism.'

The beta-carbolines are not the only hallucinogens that the pineal gland controls or affects. The main function of the gland appears to be the manufacture and release of melatonin, a hormone that works in opposition to another hormone, serotonin, which is also found in large amounts in the pineal gland, to control our day and night rhythms. Melatonin concentrations are highest at night, serotonin during the day. They counterbalance each other to give us a body clock which distinguishes day and night. (Incidentally, if we live in complete darkness our body rhythms will function normally but if we live in constant daylight they will be disrupted, leading to feelings of disorientation. For some unknown reason, if we live for a few days or more without any access to daylight or other artificial mechanisms for measuring time, we will slip into a twenty-five hour daily rhythm.)

The serotonin, which is found in concentrations fifty times greater in the pineal gland than any other part of the brain, can be converted into a chemical which is known to be an hallucinogen.

Serotonin is stored in 'synaptic vesicles' in the brain. A synapse is a junction between two nerves and a synaptic vesicle is a bubble of hormone or compound stored at one side of the junction, ready to float across and stimulate the other side. If the brain is able to register and be influenced by quantum effects, it probably happens in these synapses. Serotonin may also be responsible for that familiar feeling of 'butterflies in the stomach' when we are nervous or excited and the stronger churning of the stomach when we are afraid – both serotonin and melatonin are found in the gut, the melatonin possibly being needed to calm us down after the serotonin has caused contractions of the stomach muscles.

Melatonin's main function (or the one we can most easily define) is that it makes us drowsy after dark. It may also open us up to psi – the semi-trance we go into just before falling asleep is a prime time for psychic experiences and dreams are often psychically significant. Here, again, there are links with folklore and mystical beliefs: the early hours of the morning are popular times for meditation, which seems to attract psychic awareness; and ancient legends and folk tales connect the hours of darkness with 'magic' and witchcraft.

Peak levels of melatonin are found at 2 a.m. and some research has found that we dream more at this time. Giving extra melatonin and another hormone from the pineal gland to a group of young boys sent them immediately to sleep and caused them to dream within fifteen minutes. Babies and small children dream a lot and they have higher concentrations of melatonin than adults. There is also some evidence that up to about the age of seven or eight young children are more receptive to psi than their elders.

Work on the pineal gland is still in its early stages so some of the information that has been collected still seems scrappy and uncoordinated. However, enough is known for us to be able to see that this small gland, no bigger than the tip of your little finger, may play a very large role in much of our natural functioning and may eventually be central to our understanding of psychic abilities.

7
The Unbelievers

Psychic researchers may have been struggling to prove scientifically the existence of psi; but one theory that they have proved unintentionally along the way is that for every action you get a reaction. Their very existence, and their quest, has spawned a growing counter movement: the sceptics.

Organized groups of disbelievers call themselves Skeptics, spelt with a 'k' – an American spelling. Just as America has been the home of the most intensive parapsychological research of the last half century so, naturally, it was the birthplace of orchestrated opposition. There have always been plenty of outspoken critics of paranormal belief but today there are properly constituted groups who are dedicated to ridiculing anything to do with the supernatural.

They have had some successes. When Uri Geller was at the height of his popularity in 1974, the *Daily Mail* did a poll of its readers and discovered that ninety-five per cent of them believed Geller had paranormal powers. Although no comparable survey has been done in recent times, the continual debunking of Geller that has gone on since then will have substantially reduced that percentage.

The standard bearer of scepticism – and the man who seems to be locked in permanent battle with Geller – is James Randi, a Canadian-born magician who took offence at Geller and others using what he believes are conjuring and stage magic tricks similar to those that he and other entertainers use and passing them off as 'psychic powers'.

Randi, who gave the word 'charlatan' as his profession for his American Express card, realized when in his twenties that he could mimic telepathy, clairvoyance and precognition successfully. His real name is Randall Zwinge but, understandably, he dubbed himself the Amazing Randi for his stage shows.

It was in the early 1970s, when he was in his mid-forties, that he started to expand his stage act by including his own commentary on the paranormal and was first invited to lecture on this subject at colleges and schools. He says that he found this very satisfying because he was informing his audience as well as entertaining them. His lectures invariably include some demonstrations of conjuring, as an illustration of how easily we are all fooled by what we think we see. (He also found it rather easier to take only a briefcase with him to give a lecture, than to have a large van full of equipment for a magic show.)

Interest in him and his name grew. The Committee for the Scientific Investigation of Claims of the Paranormal was founded, and in 1986 Randi was given a $270,000 grant from a prestigious private foundation, the MacArthur Foundation, to carry on proselytizing his disbelief. One of his famous victories was Project Alpha, when he trained a couple of 'pseudo-psychics' and arranged to have them tested by parapsychologists. They took part in experiments for three years, on and off and, although the scientists never declared that the two were psychic, they never caught them cheating and their continued interest in them suggested that they thought they were genuine. When Randi made his hoax public he sealed his unpopularity with the parapsychologists.

Randi has published ten books and his name was established in Britain with a series of peak-time half-hour programmes put out by Granada in the summer of 1991 aimed at debunking the claims of mediums, psychic surgeons, dowsers, aura readers and assorted other 'psychics'. (Unfortunately for Randi, the programmes were so short and tried to cover so many subjects, that the end result was scrappy and left a lot of viewers with sympathy for the psychics who were dealt with so hastily. It could have been better television: it could also have been better at putting across Randi's message.)

He gathers a lot of publicity by carrying around in his pocket a cheque for $10,000 which he says he will give to the first person who successfully demonstrates to him the existence of paranormal abilities. He does not expect to ever have to pay it out, although he says he would be delighted to do so if he ever were satisfied by a demonstration.

'That would be an exciting moment in my life and worth every cent of my $10,000, believe me. I am certainly prepared for a demonstration of paranormal abilities – but I think it is extremely unlikely. Put it this way: I have been sitting by my chimney for years now and all my evidence tells me that Santa Claus is unlikely to appear on Christmas Eve, or any other day of the year. On the other hand, should a fat man in a red suit come down my chimney on 24 December, by golly, I'll give him my list and tell him that I have been a very good boy.'

Randi's critics assert that his confidence that his $10,000 will never be claimed stems from his insistence on certain conditions for any demonstrations. Understandably, he wants to control the experimental protocols but his critics claim that he also wants to have sole control over publishing the results and records. The psychics who submit to Randi's scrutiny must agree, if they fail, to accept that they do not possess paranormal powers. Some psychics say this excludes them from testing, because their psi powers are elusive and cannot be turned on and off at will. They compare it with testing an athlete – because he does not clear the high jump bar today does not mean that he did not do it last week or will not do it next week. Randi's critics also are concerned that he gives no guarantee not to interfere with the psychics while they are performing. This, they claim, makes a true evaluation of their powers impossible (some mediums claim that physical injury and even death can result from being disturbed while in a trance).

Randi's most public battle has been with Uri Geller, with whom he has been embroiled in litigation. Geller is the

Israeli 'super-psychic' who came to fame in the 1970s, when his astonishing feats of metal bending and other psychokinesis left audiences on several continents gasping. The debunking started almost simultaneously, with articles in magazines about the possibilities of achieving the same effect by simple sleight of hand and conjuring. Randi produced a book, *The Magic of Uri Geller*, in 1975, and the two have been at daggers drawn ever since. The legal battle between them revolves around personal allegations that Randi is claimed to have made about Geller, rather than about his disputed psychic powers. (Geller has never sued anyone for saying that he is not psychic.) The legal dispute caused Randi to resign from CSICOP, because he does not want the organization financially crippled by costly litigation.

Despite his evangelical approach and his high public profile, Randi has no desire to legislate against psychics and supporters of the paranormal. Even though, like most sceptics, he is concerned about the physical risks to believers in faith healing, he sees his role only as an educator.

'In a position of power and influence, I would seek only to use my powers to educate people. I'm just a man walking down the street who sees someone being hit by a car and knocked into the street. I'm neither a lawyer nor a medical person but I can summon the appropriate help – I drag the person out of the way of the traffic and I make sure that medical assistance is summoned and perhaps also legal assistance – but that's the most I can do. If that person wants to crawl back into the traffic to get run over a second time, I may even go after him a second time and drag him out of the traffic. But if he gets angry with me and says "I would rather be run over, thank you," I'll say, "That's your choice," and walk on my way – but not without at least attempting to summon legitimate assistance for the person. That's essentially what I'm doing, I see these people being "run down", I go over and pick them up and say "You've been run down by forces beyond your ability to control and I want to arm you so that you can control them and understand them in the future." But if they say

"Sorry, I don't want to know about it" then I simply leave them and go on my way.

'I wouldn't want to use legislation to prevent people feeling the way they want to feel and doing what they want to do as long as it doesn't harm other people. I think people should have the right to be stupid if they want to be – because among all that range of things that I class as stupid there may be lurking a new discovery.'

Randi is not the only sceptic to have taken potshots at Geller, who has become something of a fall guy for the psychics. (Many believers in psi are not believers in Geller and feel aggrieved that the question of his authenticity is paraded as the sum total of the psi debate.) Geller has set himself up for it by claiming that he has undergone – and passed – laboratory tests on his powers and that he has been employed by governments and industrialists to help them, either by influencing the minds of their opponents or by helping discover underground mineral resources. He has also been party to claims that he gained his 'psychic' powers from extra-terrestrial beings, who took him over when he was three years old: not guaranteed to win him support, except at the irrational fringes of psi belief.

There have also been claims and counter-claims from ex-members of his staff that he uses signals from confederates. One sceptic even advanced the hypothesis that he has a minute radio receiver embedded in one of his teeth, through which he gets information from members of his entourage. Geller *has* been tested in laboratories but critics like David Marks and Richard Kammann, two academics who studied him closely and wrote their own book, *The Psychology of the Psychic*, believe that he was able to dupe the scientists. After all, they ask, why should scientists be any better than anyone else at spotting deception?

It was Russell Targ and Harold Puthoff of the Stanford Research Institute who tested Geller's ESP abilities. They isolated Geller in a double-walled sealed room and asked him to duplicate drawings that were done by the experimenters in remote positions around the laboratory. In ten out of thirteen cases, they reported that Geller produced a drawing very similar to the target. Two independent judges marked the results and were able to match the drawings to the targets without error. The probability of this happening by chance is only one in three million.

They also tested Geller with dice. A three-quarter-inch-square dice was put in a steel box measuring 3" × 4" × 5". The box was shaken. Geller was asked to say which face of the dice was uppermost. In ten tries, he passed twice, but got the other eight right – which would only happen by chance once in a million. Targ and Puthoff concluded that he had demonstrated scientifically the existence of ESP.

Randi put forward his explanation of the dice experiment in his book: Geller, he said, peeped inside the box. This may seem like a farfetched claim when the experiment was operated under supposedly stringent laboratory controls but when Marks and Kammann assessed the controls they were not convinced that they were stringent enough. At first sight, the experiments look foolproof. The experimenters provided all the equipment. (One sceptic suggested the dice was radio controlled by minute equipment inside it but this was easily refuted because the dice was transparent and because Geller was not allowed access to it before the experiment.) In the drawing experiment, Targ and Puthoff eliminated clever guesswork of routine drawings (houses, trees, cats and so on) by choosing subjects at random from a dictionary. They also stated that Geller was 'at all times visually, acoustically and electrically shielded from person-nel and material in the target location'. But it is extremely difficult to deal with Uri Geller in a straightforward scientific way. He is restless and temperamental, given to walking away if he does not like the situation. All these characteristics can be put down to his highly-developed psi – or they could be put down, Marks and Kammann would argue, to essential distractions needed for his conjuring tricks to work.

The explanation, as supplied by Randi, of how he might have accomplished his good scores with the dice, was that Geller was flipping open the lid and peeping inside when he was putting his hands over the metal box to help him 'read' the dice. According to the experimenters, he had his hands on the box for some of the eight successful readings but not all, and he never picked it up.

By Geller's own admission, they would sometimes sit around for hours with nothing happening when he was being tested in the laboratory. Then, suddenly, he would feel like performing and jump up and do so. Marks and Kammann believe that in the confusion of this sudden activity, and allowing that he is a master at sleight of hand, he might have been able to cheat. The experimenters, Targ and Puthoff, claimed that magicians monitored videos of Geller performing and could find no evidence of trickery. It was later revealed that the magicians were Targ himself, an amateur; another amateur who was a regular consultant to the laboratory and an acknowledged believer in psi; and a professional magician who, according to Marks and Kammann, a few months after viewing videos of the experiments, denounced Geller as 'nothing more than a trickster', and claimed any good magician could duplicate Geller's successes.

Marks and Kammann have suggested several explanations for the drawings that Geller appeared to produce and have found weaknesses in the reported experiment. First, they believe, with some evidence, that the data was 'polished' to select the best to fit the theory. Second, Geller 'passed' or said he was unable to perform, or only performed as well as chance, when the drawing was sealed in an envelope. Third, the experiment was conducted by a team of psychologists (not Targ and Puthoff). His successes came when the drawing was displayed in one room and Geller was left alone in another. The double-walled steel room offered some possibilities for cheating: there was a hole where cables were fed through for video equipment although, according to the experimenters, the hole had a metal cover; there was a darkened window which had been covered with a bulletin board; and there was a two-way intercom system which allowed someone in the steel room to talk to the outside world. All of these provided possible ways for Geller to obtain information from an accomplice: and at least one of his close associates was around for all the tests. Although Marks and Kammann cannot be sure exactly how Geller could have cheated on each drawing, they have come up with a scenario that explains convincingly enough why some of his 'hits' were near perfect and why others were very approximate. When the example was a picture of a devil, Geller provided nothing but a badly-drawn trident to suggest the devil. Marks and Kammann believe he could have added this without the experimenters spotting him doing so, after the experiment was over. He would have been unable to look at what he was drawing which, they say, accounts for the poor image.

Geller's most famous psychic phenomena are his metal-bending activities. The fact that he can bend metal to order for television cameras belies his own claim that his powers do not work all the time, which he used to explain some of the long delays experienced in the laboratory. His metal bending was not tested at the Stanford Research Institute: Targ and Puthoff believed that because he needed physical contact with the spoon or other object, it would be impossible to monitor his feats in the lab. The sceptics claim that he bends the metal by physical strength when cameras and eyes are not on him, then deceives his audience into believing they witnessed him doing it.

He has a good track record for mending watches and clocks, but professional clock repairers say that half the broken watches and clocks they see only need cleaning and oiling, and that handling them could thin the oil and make them work, albeit only for a short time. So, too, could the shaking they get as a result of being handled. When Marks and Kammann organized an experiment, using non-psychic students to hold the broken watches, they got a success rate comparable to Geller's.

The sceptics are convinced that Geller is nothing more than an accomplished stage magician. In fact, as Marks and Kammann say:

'Geller is the only performing magician today whose public image goes up by failures, becauses they help convince people that he is *not* a magician.'

Paul Daniels, himself no slouch as a magician, does not

believe that Geller is psychic, but equally does not believe there is any harm in Geller's act.

'He's a great showman. I don't know where you draw the line. I mean, if people say that he is a con artist, to what extent is he a con artist? Who has he conned? He has entertainment value but, in my view, he has no psychic powers whatever. I don't believe that he can bend metal by thought waves – or do anything else by thought waves. He's a good entertainer, if you leave it at that.'

Daniels is outspokenly sceptical about all paranormal claims, although he admits than in his youth he believed in telepathy.

'I believed that it was probable that people could transmit thought waves to one another. I believed in religious mysticism and I thought, therefore, that as an extension of transmitting thought waves, telekinesis might be possible. I used to sit for hours trying to move a ping-pong ball across a table. It was only when I could afford a wider range of books that I became a lot more logical and a lot more observant,' he told *The Skeptic* magazine.

Daniels once went to the trouble to experiment with astrology. He got a typist to re-type the star sign information from an astrology book and switch the headings around. When people he met asked about astrology he told them he was preparing a book, asked them their star sign and then showed them the piece marked with that sign. They all felt it was a good assessment of their character.

He repudiates the accusation, from the psychic world, that he has a negative attitude. He says he would love to meet someone who had paranormal powers.

'If I could find somebody who could really do magic, really bend metal, I'd put him on my television programme. On the other hand, if you really had that power would you want to spend your life bending spoons? To say I'm negative is a joke. I want to meet a real psychic. I want to meet a ghost. And I would be prepared to pay. Even now, with all the knowledge and reading that's in my head, I'd really like to meet one.'

Daniels' stand against the paranormal is not necessarily

typical of all professional magicians and conjurers. A survey at a magicians' convention in America showed that over fifty per cent believed in some aspects of the paranormal. The figure is lower than in the population in general where seventy per cent believe in some form of telepathy or clairvoyance but, interestingly, it was higher among the 'mentalists', the magicians who specialize in faking telepathy. 'I think that is because they are in a continuing situation where they are trying to reproduce mental powers and occasionally things happen that they haven't planned for – their trick happens without trying,' said Richard Wiseman.

Wiseman is a young psychology graduate who has done his PhD at the Koestler Parapsychology Department of Edinburgh University, studying 'strategies of deception'. He is uniquely qualified because from the age of twelve he has been a practising magician and helped finance his way through university by working as one professionally. He has lectured to magicians on the need to co-operate in sharing their techniques with parapsychologists and to parapsychologists on the need to clue themselves up far more about the ways in which they can be deceived. He is astonished that, bending a key in front of a distinguished gathering of parapsychologists, there were many who expressed amazement and wonder at his ability to perform the trick. 'They of all people should be aware of trickery. I'm not saying they should all know how it is done, but they should all accept that a convincing demonstration of metal bending is likely to be nothing more than a trick. They should be more sceptical.'

The Skeptics movement in Britain (they say they choose the American spelling because it precludes mispronunciation as 'septic', and because it is an old English spelling) has no recognizable figurehead like Randi. Although Paul Daniels, Stephen Fry, Jonathan Miller and Patrick Moore are all outspoken sceptics, full-time debunking would obviously be a tremendous commitment. British sceptics have the bi-monthly *Skeptic* magazine, which sells between five hundred and a thousand copies, mainly to members of Skeptic groups. The editors, Toby Howard and Steve Donnelly, both university lecturers, acknowledge that the magazine is circulating predominantly to those who are already sceptics. They would like to see it have a more general readership.

'We know we are preaching to the converted: we'd like to reach far more people who have never been supplied with enough facts to make up their minds about it all. There are lots of floating voters: people with an interest in the subject. But the only information they have on which to base their opinions is the mish-mash of bits and pieces they read about in newspapers or magazines.'

Dr Donnelly acknowledges that their evangelical zeal for scepticism is hard to understand.

'I realize it may seem to many people strange to give up our spare time to this, when there are more important problems on the planet, such as starvation in Africa. But, I suppose, everybody latches on to something. Many people will reject the paranormal without feeling that it is harmful to others who do believe in it, or that it merits actually getting up and trying to convert others to their point of view. We feel that belief in strange and unproven things is not a good way for a society to progress.

'The American sceptics investigated astrology and came to the conclusion that there was nothing in it but that it was harmless and a damn sight cheaper than going to an analyst. I'm not so sure it is harmless, I think it may lead on to a whole set of paranormal beliefs.

'If society in a large way came to depend on divine guidance – consulting palmists, astrologers, mediums and the like every week – we would begin to lose any sense of being responsible for ourselves, we would be putting our destinies in the hands of random factors. I want to see individuals empowered, given back responsibility for themselves, not made dependent.

'As a university lecturer I see myself as an educator and I think we should be educating our young people better in the ways of rational thinking. If they were taught about the wonders and mysteries of their own universe they would not need the mysteries of Doris Collins or their star sign.'

Dr Donnelly believes unequivocally that the psychical researchers and parapsychologists have totally failed to prove the existence of psi. He has a lot of respect for the parapsychologists, acknowledging that many of them are dedicated and sincere scientists.

'I don't believe their research will ever bear fruit, but there are plenty of people in orthodox areas of science who will devote a whole lifetime researching an area that will never bear fruit. Professor Morris and his team at Edinburgh are meticulous and serious, I have no problems with them. But I suspect that some parapsychologists see what they are looking for in their research, because they are believers in psi (just as in other areas of science you get individuals who make their results fit their theories).

'Obviously, I haven't monitored every single research paper produced by the parapsychologists. But, in all the cases I can think of where there have been positive results, it is unclear whether the proper controls were in place when the experiments were carried out.

'When the early crusaders of the SPR were looking at paranormal things, they were investigating areas that the man in the street would regard as significant: ghosts, poltergeists, mediums. Now the academics have moved into the refined area of statistics, and I don't believe the man in the street would find even their best results at all impressive.

'Although I may not agree with their conclusions, I do not think there is anything harmful about their work.'

As a physicist, Dr Donnelly acknowledges the siren call of the quantum mechanics theory of the paranormal (see chapter 6).

'It makes interesting reading and it is hard to dismiss it completely. It can appear to be an impressive explanation of any disorderly event. The theory of uncertainty gets pushed up into macroscopic objects and gets applied to the workings of the brain.

'But the truth, I fear, is that the theorists have constructed a rational framework, then made one irrational leap, and put a rational construction on the other side of the leap. In this case, the irrational leap is to believe that a macroscopic area like the brain can be affected by micro events. In physics, quantum mechanics has made its impact in short timescales, small dimensions. When you move into big systems you don't see the effects of quantum mechanics. Newtonian physics is adequate to describe things, unless you are dealing with objects moving near the speed of light.

'It is not hard for renegade physicists to convince intelligent lay people of their theories. The average person has very little knowledge of science: we teach it so badly. As a scientist, I am still able to appreciate art and literature (perhaps not at quite the same level as my friends who have studied it for degrees, but none the less, I'm not completely thrown by it). Most of science is inaccessible to lay people. That's not a comment on their intellect: they have not been given the tools to understand it. So when a scientist comes along with a belief system to push, he can easily blind and subvert his lay audience. The other scientists, the majority who would repudiate his theory, have no motivation to get out there and put forward their views.'

Like many other sceptics, Dr Donnelly's opinions were shaped through an initial belief in the paranormal and an expectation of being able to test it, followed by the realization that he was consistently failing to find evidence.

'I was convinced that I had a telepathic relationship with my mum. My conviction was based on experiences like one when we both, quite separately, bought an identical (and unusual) gift for someone we knew. At first that seemed very unlikely and proof that we were telepathic. Then I thought about it. I spent the first eighteen years of my life living with my mother, half my genes came from her, we have similar taste. It's not so surprising that we made the same choice and, when the telepathy between us should have worked, when my aunt died while I was away in Russia without my mother being able to contact me (an event which upset my mother a great deal) I didn't receive any telepathic messages.

'By and large, believers in the paranormal only remember the bits that fit their belief. They remember the matching gifts, not the lack of telepathy at a crucial time. Recently, I had what could be described as a classic premonitory dream. I was standing on a plane runway in my dream and I saw a large plane coming in to land with its engine on fire. It flew over my shoulder and burst into flames on impact with the runway. I saw it clearly: it was a turquoise blue colour.

'Now, it happens that after my dream there were no air crashes reported from anywhere in the world for over two months, which is unusual. If there had been one within a few days of my dream, I might well have convinced myself that was the one I dreamed about, even though it did not match my dream in detail. Subconsciously, the dream would change to fit the facts of the reported crash and the whole experience would become very significant to me. A colleague of mine, a complete sceptic, was driving down the motorway when he suddenly had very acute indigestion pains – he did not normally suffer from indigestion. He found out later that his father had died at roughly the same time as he was having the attack and he is now convinced that it was a telepathic communication.'

When the first great flurry of interest in Uri Geller hit Britain in the 1970s, Dr Donnelly was a student member of the SPR. At that time, he was doing some laboratory work using a microbalance which measured in micrograms. He devised an experiment in which he tried to influence the balance through the power of thought: nothing happened.

Dr Donnelly's biggest worries are in the area of faith healing and, particularly, psychic surgery, where he believes that actual physical harm can be inflicted on people. He would like to see the law tightened to prevent anyone setting up in practice as a healer without proper safeguards and qualifications. EC regulations will help, but he would like to see more.

'I am not dismissing all alternative medicine. Some of the

psychological aspects of it can help people to feel that they are helping themselves. But it is very dangerous if patients come to rely on it. This already happens in America, with victims turning down antibiotics in favour of herbal remedies that do nothing.'

He and his fellow sceptics are now crusading to have their case aired more regularly and more fairly – they reckon they get a bad deal from the media, who latch on to sensational reports of the paranormal and are not too interested in presenting the other side. (Interestingly, the parapsychologists claim that only sceptics can get articles about the paranormal published in prestigious scientific journals; and many serious psychic researchers also complain about the reluctance of the media to take their viewpoint seriously.)

'The lot of presenting a rationalist, sceptical view is not a happy one: people see us as spoil sports. They want to believe in something mysterious and magical. We don't want to stop people having fun. In America, some newspapers and magazines carry a box alongside the astrology column which says that it is for entertainment only. A lot of serious astrologers, as well as sceptics, think this is a step forward. We would not like to see stars columns banned. After all, even a sceptic knows his own sign – I'm Aries. I think it's all rather silly and I don't bother to read it, but it's perfectly harmless as long as everyone knows it is only fun.'

Dr Donnelly's conversion to scepticism from an initial belief in psi, largely because of the failure of his own experiments to demonstrate a paranormal effect, is mirrored by the case of Dr Sue Blackmore, the original poacher turned gamekeeper of the British sceptic scene. Her defection to the ranks of the sceptics was significant, because she was one of the most active parapsychologists in the country (amongst many other things she was the editor of the SPR journal). She still is active: her fascination with the subject has not diminished, though her convictions have changed. This, she says, makes her unpopular with both sides.

'I get criticism from everybody. As far as the believers are concerned I'm bad because I'm sceptical, I challenge people, I come forward and state my failure to get good experimental results. As far as the sceptics are concerned, I'm bad because I'm interested in mystical things, I spend my time researching near death experiences and out of body experiences.

'Although I don't believe in the paranormal, there are obviously lots of phenomena for which at present we don't have full and complete explanations, and so the research must continue. I believe we will find good mystical, psychological, and even physical, explanations of everything eventually.

'I think it is sad that so much money has been withdrawn from serious parapsychology in recent years. Today, it is easier to get rich people to give money to fund what they see as science versus the irrational – in other words, the sceptics' cause is popular at the moment. The whole field of parapsychology is shrinking terribly and some sceptics are pleased, but I'm not. What we need, above all, are good researchers and there are some excellent researchers among the believers. They come into the field because of their belief, but they do not let their belief cloud their scientific conclusions.

'So in many ways I am between the two camps. I am sceptical but, at the same time, I believe we should encourage and support the research, because although it may never land us with proof of the paranormal it will lead to a fuller and better understanding of many things.'

Dr Blackmore's interest in the subject was seriously aroused when she was a student at Oxford. She believed she had had paranormal experiences: she noted strings of coincidences, read tarot cards and was convinced they worked, felt she could communicate telepathically with her boyfriend.

'I wanted to track down the paranormal, because I believed we would understand the whole of psychology by understanding the paranormal. So, at Oxford, I found myself running the university's Psychical Research Society and I became very enthusiastic. At that time, I would say I was an eighty-five per cent believer; now I am an eighty-five per cent disbeliever. It is not possible to disbelieve one hundred per cent because it is impossible to prove psi is not there, all we can ever say is that we have not found any evidence for it.'

It was her out of body experience (see chapter 4) that confirmed her belief but, twenty years later, she is able to explain the reasons she believed it happened to her.

'I was very, very tired, I'd partly smoked a joint, not a lot but enough to make me woozy, I'd spent four or five hours on the ouija board. I really did believe it was my astral body up there on the ceiling and I was convinced that it was evidence that we survive death.'

It was only after Oxford, when she was working for her PhD and carrying out controlled experiments to try to find psi, that Dr Blackmore began slowly to question her own beliefs.

'I believed that ESP and memory were aspects of the same thing, that telepathy simply meant tapping into collective memories on behalf of someone else. So I spent three years devising experiments to find out in what ways ESP and memory were similar – and failed because I failed to find any ESP. After five years working on my PhD, I was very sceptical.'

She tackled ganzfeld experiments (probably the area of research most frequently acclaimed by parapsychologists as a successful demonstration of psi). She found no evidence that sensory deprivation heightened psi awareness – again, she found no psi at all. She sparked a controversy by saying so and by criticizing the standards of controls used by other researchers.

'I did not have the opportunity to do lots of experiments, nor to monitor in detail everything else that had been done but, from starting out with the belief that the ganzfeld area looked good, I ended up suspecting that the research might be deeply flawed.'

Dr Blackmore also tried without success to replicate some research which seemed to establish that young children are highly psychic. It has been a long-held theory that we are all born psychic, and that the process of growing up in a culture that rejects psi causes us to close down our receptors and inhibit our natural abilities. It follows from this that young children, too young to have been 'nobbled' by society, should be more psychic than adults. There were experiments that seemed to confirm this, with three-years-olds scoring the highest: but when Susan Blackmore tried similar experiments she failed to obtain the same results. Her three-year-old subjects guessed the colour of Smarties at exactly the level they would be expected to by chance.

Again, she found herself in dispute with the findings of others. Dr Blackmore says she also realized that her tarot readings were good because she had become adept at picking up clues from the subjects to whom she was giving the readings. Again, her views were controversial: some researchers believe that her own results are proof positive of a psi effect, even though she herself denies it.

'The tarot cards are a wonderful map of human nature, brilliantly devised. In the right hands, they're a good psychotherapeutic tool, they can deliver really good insights into human nature. But I believe it is necessary for the person doing the reading to reflect the feedback they get from the subject. In other words, when the cards are dealt blind, without contact between the reader and the subject, they offer no particular insights. It is bogus to claim that they reflect the cosmos: they are just a good way to get into talking about things, to open the subject up. When I experimented with blind readings, the subjects could not select their own reading from among ten others.'

As part of her work for the SPR, and also because she is known from her television and radio broadcasts to be knowledgeable on the subject, Dr Blackmore has over the years studied several individual cases of the 'paranormal'.

'People who have heard about me just get in touch. One man recently brought a windowsill to show me – he could see in the wood a picture of the Virgin Mary, the donkey and Jesus himself. I could see the patterns myself: the wood was very grainy and full of different shapes, some looking like faces. I explained to him that it is a natural human instinct to look for faces in patterns: the first thing a baby recognizes is a face and we continue to seek out faces for the rest of our lives.

'He believed God had given him the windowsill for a reason. I managed to persuade him that God said he did not want any graven images, and that the man should perhaps just take it as a sign that he should be more Christian in his own life. I tried not to be too negative, but I made it clear that I did not believe in religion.'

She tested a dowser using a map of the grounds of the university, on which she had marked all the underground water, electricity, gas and sewerage services. Although he told her about an underground chamber five thousand feet down in the ground, and therefore impossible to confirm or deny, he failed to pick up the known water conduits.

The only interesting poltergeist that Dr Blackmore has investigated appeared in a Bristol council house. It was referred to her by the local Unidentified Flying Objects group, who had started to look into the case but, because the woman involved was having out of body experiences, seeing apparitions, and the whole family was witnessing strange phenomena, passed it over to Dr Blackmore.

'By the time I visited the house it was a classic poltergeist outburst. Lights would swing, doors would open and close, the kettle switched itself on and off, there were noises of the toilet roll holder being rattled when nobody was in the bathroom. The most persistent phenomena were the TV, which kept switching channels by itself, and the clock, which moved on its own along the mantelpiece.

'I went to the house once a week for several months, and got the residents to keep a detailed diary of events. I had the television looked at by an electronics expert, who discovered that, although it did not have a remote control channel selector, it had been fitted with a receiving device for a remote selector. This could be triggered by high-pitched sounds. For instance, if we rattled the dog's chain we could get the telly to change channels.

'Then, one day, I actually saw the clock move. It skipped about an inch along the mantelpiece. I wanted to find out whether the "power" that made it behave like that was in the clock or in the house, so I took the clock away with me and put it on my desk at home. It continued to move. I gave it to a technician at Bristol University, where I was working. Clocks and watches were his hobby. He took it to pieces and found that it was a light, metal 1950s clock with a very heavy old-fashioned spring inside. The spring was clogged up with dirt and so was unwinding unevenly, causing the clock to jerk. It would not have happened if the clock had been heavier – and it didn't happen when the clock was cleaned.

'When these two major aspects of the activity had been sorted out, the rest just faded away. Until then, the whole family had talked about 'Mr Poltie', and I think they were noticing what were nothing more than normal things – a light swinging in a sudden breeze, a door clicking open or closed on its own, a kettle that someone had forgotten that they had already switched on. Everything was ascribed to Mr Poltie. When his main skills – the telly and the clock – were taken from him, he ceased to exist.

'The woman still had out of body experiences and I tried to get her to harness and control them – but she lost interest.

'In almost all poltergeist cases you can find problems in the family somewhere. But then, you can find problems in any family: no controlled studies have been done.

'The Rosenheim case seems to be a good one, but I'm not sure I would accept it as evidence that the world is not what it seems to be. I know people who went there and were very impressed, and others who were not impressed at all. The Cardiff case also looks impressive: but I don't believe enough controls have been set in place to eliminate other explanations. Tony Cornell's apparatus should be used: if it finds fraud, you know what you are up against. If it does not, you still cannot rule out other explanations but at least they are not obvious. It is better than nothing.

'The Enfield case is a puzzle. It was Maurice Grosse's first case: he may have missed things that a more experienced investigator would have picked up.

'One of the problems for the SPR in farming out cases is that ninety-nine per cent of them come to nothing and they cannot tell which are going to be the exciting ones.'

Dr Blackmore's main areas of research are crisis visions and out of body experiences (see chapter 4). She has also been carrying out experiments to test her theory that it is those among us who are the least able judges of probability who are the most likely to believe in the paranormal – in other words, those who miscalculate how likely events are to happen spontaneously are liable to ascribe them to the paranormal. Most of us do assess probability rather poorly.

As a test, answer these four questions:

1 A hat contains ten red and ten blue Smarties. I pull out ten and eight of them are red. Which colour am I more likely to get next?
2 A box contains green and yellow buttons in unknown proportions. I pull out ten and eight are yellow. Which colour am I more likely to get next?
3 Two football teams have met four times and the same team has won the toss each time. When they meet for the fifth time, which is more likely to win the toss?
4 How many people would you need at a party to have an even chance of two of them sharing the same birthday (not counting the year of birth).

The answers are blue; yellow; they have an equal chance; and twenty-two.

This last is the most likely to raise eyebrows. If we increase the number of people at the party to forty-eight, we have a ninety-five per cent chance of two of them sharing the same birthday.

Surprised? Even more surprising is the statistical analysis done by Christopher Scott on the classic 'psychic' dream, when a person dreams of the death of someone who they later discovered died that night. By computing the number of deaths in Britain each day, the population of Britain, and the assumption that each one will have a dream about the death of someone they know just once in their lifetime, he concludes that about once every two weeks someone somewhere in Britain dreams a dream that actually coincides with the death of the subject. It seems tremendously significant to the dreamer, but is in fact not that unlikely.

Although Dr Blackmore's research has appeared to support her theory that the worst judges of probability are the biggest believers in psi, one experiment has contradicted this, so she is wary about drawing conclusions.

'All I know is that "psychic" experiences are not as rare or as significant as we think they are. And I still feel sure that those who believe in psi will be more likely to interpret unusual events as being paranormal, rather than looking for other explanations or accepting that chance played a major part in it.'

Although he puts himself at the other end of the paranormal belief scale, Professor Bob Morris from Edinburgh University approaches his research in a very similar way to Dr Blackmore. His 'benign scepticism' has led him to produce a programme of research at Edinburgh that is at least as biased towards eliminating potential fraud and unintentional deception as it is to establishing the existence of psi.

'Faking has been big business for thousands of years, either for financial reasons or for social or personal influence. That is why we study the psychology of deception, specifically looking at how our background and attitudes and understanding of the world influence what we observe. The more we know about deception and how it operates, the more we can equip ourselves with tools to assess claims of the paranormal. We need to know what questions to ask people, what observations to make.'

There are five basic ways in which observers can be deceived:

1 They may be given inaccurate information
2 They may be led to misperceive the information
3 Their attention may be diverted
4 They may be led to misinterpret the information
5 They may be led to misremember the information

In each case, the deception could be deliberate, as in faking or fraud, or it could be done by the observer to themselves: in other words, they deceive themselves. The researcher, when interviewing people about their experiences, has to guard not just against the likelihood that they have been deceived, but that by his own questioning he loads the answers. For instance, if it's clear from the questions asked that the researcher is looking for a certain result, the person being questioned may, out of politeness, give him the answers he wants, or conversely may resist them. Having the magician Richard Wiseman working at Edinburgh has given the team there a good opportunity to study the nature of deception. Volunteers are shown magic tricks, and then asked about what they recall. The specific details they single out can be cross-related to their basic attitudes. His work with parapsychologists has not convinced Wiseman of the existence of psi – he remains resolutely non-committal about the possibility of it really existing.

'If pushed, I am more of a goat than a sheep. But that does not mean I rule it out. I've never encountered it, but then I have not been out in the field looking for it. I have been concerned with establishing a methodology, a means of knowing when people are cheating, rather than testing individuals, which is time consuming. Now that we have established some sort of methodology I hope I will be able to spend more time on actual cases.'

Richard Wiseman has concentrated on studying 'macro-PK' – fake physical mediumship in particular, and metal bending.

'Although the techniques for bending a spoon and levitating a table are different, the way observers are deceived into not seeing the cheating that is going on is similar.

'I am no expert on the paranormal. There are whole chunks of it that I know nothing about. All I'm trying to do is frame some system that we can test people under, given that we know that they may cheat. There's a tremendous motivation for so-called psychics to cheat in the laboratory. They would get tremendous kudos – and maybe even great financial rewards – if they could promote themselves as having being scientifically verified as psychic. They would also get great satisfaction in just getting one over on the parapsychologists or whoever was testing them.'

Wiseman does not believe that all cheating should automatically be treated as a bad thing. Like others working in the field he accepts that if psi exists, it is an elusive thing, and that cheating may be a precursor to the real thing.

'Some gentle cheating at the beginning can, we're told, put some people into the right frame of mind for the genuine stuff. Others, especially if they are working commercially, are compelled to cheat in order to perform on demand – their cheating does not rule out genuine abilities. So perhaps we should not be concerned with preventing cheating entirely, but simply with being aware when it is going on.'

Whereas Dr John Beloff, who is now retired and is an Honorary Fellow of Edinburgh University, agrees with Wiseman that cheating does not preclude the genuine article, Professor Morris takes an opposite view. He believes that, although guinea pigs who cheat can be used as a source of ideas no inference of psi can ever be drawn from their data: once a cheat, always a cheat. Richard Wiseman is also concerned that detecting cheating should extend beyond the laboratory.

'It is argued that psychics are unable to perform in the sterile conditions of the laboratory, and that is certainly understandable. So I believe we have to have sufficient

knowledge to be able to detect deception in other surroundings, even the surroundings of the psychic's own
choice, where the opportunities to cheat will probably be
greater.'

Before Wiseman joined the Edinburgh team they ran an
extensive series of tests on a teenager who was referred to
them by his school, because of his apparent PK abilities.
When Deborah Delanoy, one of the parapsychologists
working at Edinburgh, became suspicious, she arranged
for a secret camera to record the boy. He was caught in
an act of blatant fraud and then owned up that he had
been cheating all along.

'One of the problems in the past has been that magicians
are notoriously secretive about their techniques – and with
good reason, as it is their livelihood,' said Wiseman. 'But
whenever I have talked to groups and explained the reasons
why parapsychologists need to have a basic understanding
of their trade, they have appreciated the point.

'There are more than two thousand five hundred books
on magic in print in Britain at the moment. When we at
Edinburgh get requests from researchers who are having
problems testing certain "psychics", we can refer them to
the right book on, say, table levitation. It means that they
go into the experiments forewarned and forearmed.

'Having done this work, it is possible to look at reports
of experiments carried out by parapsychologists all over the
world and see where great holes have been left out of their
procedure, giving the guinea pig plenty of opportunity to
cheat. That doesn't mean that he or she did cheat, but it
means the research is pretty meaningless. I simply believe
that if we find out as much as we can about the ways and
means by which cheating can occur, and eliminate them,
then we can truly say that we have tested fairly.

'It is important for the psychics as well – if they really
exist. If they do, it must be very frustrating to carry out
experiments that appear to be satisfactory until someone
picks holes in the experimental procedure and accuses you
of cheating. It is in their interests, too, for the scientists to
get it right, get it foolproof.'

One area that the sceptics – and the 'benign sceptics' like Professor Morris – are all concerned about is fake mediumship. They see this as an area where financial and emotional harm can be inflicted on a gullible public.

'What really persuaded me to abandon my belief in the paranormal was going to see platform mediums at work,' said Dr Donnelly. 'They were very unimpressive – at the level of standing up in front of an audience of three hundred in Manchester and asking if anyone had recently lost an Albert.

'Many mediums are consciously deluding the public, sometimes not even for financial gain. Others, the less successful ones, are perhaps even sincere in what they are doing. I was involved in a television programme in which a medium gave some information about a motorcycle crash to a young woman in the audience, mentioning two fairly common men's names, and telling the girl that he was being told by the spirit world that she had lost an earring, and that she had a pile of untidy shoes in her wardrobe. What young girl hasn't lost an earring? They all have piles of shoes.

'Interestingly, after the programme was broadcast, the producer received phone calls from people who had been in the audience at other times when this medium had performed and the messages he had given each time were almost identical. If he's genuine, he must regard it as rather strange that the spirits who communicate with him always seem to want to tell him about lost earrings and piles of shoes. If he's not genuine, then it's a consumer con, exactly like selling washing machines that don't work.

'Mediums will argue that they help counsel people – I accept that. But I think there is a risk that they stop people grieving properly for their dead relatives, although whenever I make this point to mediums and spiritualists they insist that they do not allow people to become dependent on them. I accept that, in some ways, they do provide a service: many people are upset if someone died before they were able to apologize for something, or tell them they loved them, all sorts of things. If they believe they can do this through a medium, it probably helps.'

Dr Blackmore has not made a study of mediums, although she has visited a few and not been impressed. She believes that the majority are sincere but misguided: they are not deliberate frauds.

'Most of them are picking up cues from the sitters, without realizing what they are doing. If they say they want to hold a hand so that they can pick up vibrations, they literally are doing that – because we involuntarily signal with our hands whether something we have heard is interesting or not. We squeeze slightly when our attention is engaged and we are excited. The medium recognizes this, but does not consciously analyse it.

'I went to one who was highly recommended to me. She asked me lots of questions. When I asked the others who had been to her whether she asked them questions, they all said no, that she only told them things. We have a tendency to remember what we want to remember. For example, on Randi's television series, a man who had had a very successful reading from a medium was asked how many names she had mentioned to him. He believed it was four or five, and that they had all been right. In fact, it was about thirty, including variations on names. He only remembered the ones that were right.

'I am concerned about mediums because I believe they can prolong and delay the natural grieving process for the bereaved. If you think the person is still there you don't come to terms with them not being. I think it is particularly difficult for the brothers and sisters of a child who has died if the parents cling to the belief that the child is still there. How can any brother or sister compete with a dead rival, a rival who is always perfect and can do no wrong? It must be very disturbing for them.'

Like Dr Blackmore, Professor Morris is concerned about the ethics of fake mediumship but he is also worried about debunking: if people have built their lives on a belief, is it right to set out to pull it away from under them? He believes that the detection of fake mediums is important scientifically, but that it is important that it is not done in an atmosphere of exposure and attack.

'We have no right to pull down the belief systems of others: we simply have to make available to everyone who wants it as much information as we can about how we can be deceived.'

Chris Roe, one of his Edinburgh team, has made a study of psychic readings, and has collected the available literature offering techniques to would-be readers, reviewing other research by psychologists and sceptics. He has also talked to a confessed 'pseudo-psychic' about his *modus operandi*. It is possible to come up with lists of strategies used by both the person who goes for the reading and the client – some of them obvious, some much more subtle.

Readings are split into two groups: 'cold' and 'warm'. A cold reading is when the medium or psychic knows nothing about the client; a warm reading is when they deliberately and sometimes quite openly (although usually without the client registering it) fish for information, and get verbal feedback from the subject which helps compile an accurate personality profile. (There are also some totally unscrupulous readers who actually plant accomplices in the waiting room to extract information from waiting clients, or go through their coat pockets for clues: these are known as 'hot' readings.) If the client feels comfortable and relaxed and the reader seems friendly and sincere, a lot of information will be freely volunteered. Still more will be teased out of the client: the reader may say they are confused by what they are picking up, and ask the client to explain. Or they may ask a series of rhetorical questions, looking for confirmation or denial from the client. But a 'warm' reader will also use many of the same strategies as a cold reader. They will both use 'Barnum statements', named after the great circus showman because they are, to a large extent, another example of popular entertainment. A Barnum statement is a character assessment that the client will think refers to him or her alone: in fact, a good Barnum statement applies to eighty-five per cent of the population. For instance, telling a woman who has a wedding ring on her finger that 'family are the most important thing in your life' is not going to prompt a denial. For men a good one is: 'people may think you are tough, but deep down inside you are sensitive and can be hurt.' A list of thirteen Barnum statements was published by B.R. Forer in a psychology journal in 1949, and they still hold good today:

1 You have a great need for other people to like and admire you.
2 You have a tendency to be critical of yourself.
3 You have a great deal of unused capacity which you have not turned to your advantage.
4 While you have some personality weaknesses, you are generally able to compensate for them.
5 Your sexual adjustment has caused some problems for you.
6 Disciplined and controlled outside, you tend to worry and be insecure inside.
7 At times you have serious doubts about whether you have made the right decision or done the right thing.
8 You prefer a certain amount of change and variety and become dissatisfied when hemmed in by restrictions and limitations.
9 You pride yourself as an independent thinker, and do not accept others' statements without satisfactory proof.
10 You have found it unwise to be too frank in revealing yourself to others.
11 At times you are extroverted, affable, sociable, while at other times you are introverted, wary reserved.
12 Some of your aspirations tend to be pretty un-realistic.
13 Security is one of your major goals in life.

Some of these are double-edged, 6 and 11, for instance. They cover all options. Some allow you to read whatever you like into them, 2, for instance. Some, for example, 4 and 9, are so generally favourable that most clients accept them. There are other, more specific, statements which none the less hold true for many clients. Readers can say 'you will spot a bargain while out shopping'. This is so trivial that the client will forget it unless they do. More significantly, mentioning a male relative who died with chest pains gets a high acceptance level. Readers have to be observant and become expert at pigeon-holing people. Age is important: a young woman in her late teens or twenties will want to hear about romance; one between thirty and fifty-five will be concerned with home and children; an older woman will still want to know about family ties but illness and death will also be important topics. Clothes and accent can reveal a great deal about the financial and educational background of the client, and there may be other non-verbal clues as to state of health, happiness and so on. A glance out of the window may reveal what car they drive and, if the reading takes place in their own home, there are many clues for the reader to seize on.

Clients subdivide into roughly two groups: those who have come along out of curiosity, or for fun, and those who have a specific need. The first group can usually be satisfied with clever use of Barnum statements; the second will often reveal their need fairly early in the sitting.

When a platform medium is working in front of an audience, or if telephone or radio readings are being given, the number of clues is limited. Many of the same principles still apply and, in front of an audience, throwing out statements, a medium has a good chance of striking lucky with someone, especially as those who have paid out good money to be there will be listening hard for anything that might connect the 'message' with themselves.

Fake mediumship is such an obvious area for fraud that it is a gift to the sceptics. There are many phoney mediums making a living out of the gullible and the curious; there are many more sincere mediums (many of them operating within Spiritualist Churches and not charging any more than their bus fares) who are unwittingly deploying all or some of the techniques used by the cynical phoneys. They do not realize how they are gleaning information and genuinely believe that they are 'picking up vibrations'.

They are, but there is nothing paranormal or spiritual about those vibrations.

This does not mean that genuine mediumship does not exist. As Professor Morris says:

'After all, I can fake the symptoms of most of the world's illnesses, that does not mean the illnesses do not exist.'

8
Pay-offs

Professional gamblers know the meaning of riding their luck. They don't base their careers at the racetrack, in the gaming room or round the poker table on luck but they recognize a winning streak when it comes and they are ready to go with it, playing unerring hunches instead of following the meticulous systems that keep them ahead of the bookies and the casinos the rest of the time. Some of them seem to have more than their fair share of luck to ride. Perhaps, if they could be tested in a laboratory, they would prove to be psi stars like Matthew Manning and Malcolm Bessent.

Manning was a poltergeist agent as a boy and, as an adult, has developed automatic writing and healing skills, possibly harnessing safely whatever energy he was able to generate when he sent objects whizzing around his school dormitory. More as a joke than a serious experiment, he tried asking the spirit of his great grandfather, who was a racehorse owner, to come up with some tips for him. He was given the names of six horses: two were winners, one came second and two came third. A series of each-way bets would have netted him a nice profit. Manning has been happy to submit his healing abilities to laboratory testing and has had some success in experiments in which he tried to stop blood seeping into a saline solution. In other experiments he has influenced the growth rate of cancer cell cultures in the laboratory.

Bessent is a British businessman who has used his psi abilities only incidentally – he has followed his hunches from time to time in his business dealings – but who has been exhaustively tested in American parapsychology labs and has consistently shown psi abilities that are well above average.

Could the psi abilities of stars like these be harnessed and used in an organized and structured way? Could we all learn to develop our psi abilities so that we could run down the Grand National line-up, pick the winner and clean out the bookies? The answer to the second question is definitely no – not yet. The experiments carried out in Edinburgh to try to train and improve psi ability were not successful (or only successful in the negative way that they proved it is not yet possible). The answer to the first question, however, may be a very qualified yes. Uri Geller is one of a band of 'psychic consultants' who claim to have worked for big business and governments involved in exploration for natural resources. It is not known how successful they have been, but one can only assume that the financial constraints of business would mean that the investment would be expected to pay dividends.

When a group of three parapsychologists in America – one of them believed to be a gifted psychic – formed themselves into a business consortium in 1982 to play the market by predicting the fluctuations in the price of silver, they initially made a killing, but their second year of trading was unsuccessful. In a later experiment, $25,000 was made for charity by using the predictions of seven different psi stars.

There are other ways in which those who believe they are psychic get involved in practical work. Psychic healers abound: some of them charlatans and scoundrels, others well-meaning but ineffectual, while a few record successes that, even when psychosomatic effects are eliminated, are beyond normal explanation. Sceptics argue, with some justification, that the damage done by the phoneys far outweighs whatever genuine claims there are to cure and that this whole area needs to be regulated.

Psychics also set themselves up as detectives, usually

unpaid. When police are searching for missing bodies, or involved in big murder investigations that grab national headlines, they are frequently approached by psychics claiming to know where the body is buried or what the murderer looks like. Often these psychics are taken up by the media and, sometimes, the published information given by them can be positively misleading and consequently damaging to the police investigation. Many of them claim successes that the real detectives involved in the case would contest. Occasionally, they score genuine hits, with some uncannily correct descriptions (but more often than not these details are extracted from among a lot more that are off beam). None the less, psychic detection is beginning to be taken seriously in America, where the Institute of Parapsychology gets several phone calls every year from police officers wanting advice on whether and how to deal with psychics. Unfortunately, because no organized research has been done on the subject, there is very little advice to offer and what there is boils down to individual detectives having to make decisions about whether to put manpower into following up psychic tips. In just six months, the police involved in the 1981 Atlanta child murders case had information volunteered by one hundred and forty-six psychics, none of it helpful.

Britain's most famous 'psychic detective' is Nella Jones, who claims to have predicted the date and the city (Leeds) of the Yorkshire Ripper's last murder, as well as the victim's initials. She also says she helped track down a stolen Vermeer painting. The police are less enthusiastic about her claims but she says this is because they don't want to attract criticism. She is frequently consulted by relatives of missing people: she says she can sense whether they are still alive or not.

There have always been rumours about psi being used for military purposes by both the Russians and the Americans. Legend says that the Old Testament prophet Elisha was able to 'listen' to the plans of the Israelites' enemy, the King of Syria, by 'travelling' psychically to the King's bedchamber while battle plans were being laid there (see chapter 4).

That's not so different from what the CIA were trying to achieve in the 1970s, when they funded a programme of research into 'remote viewing', where psychics were given map references and asked to describe the locale. The series of experiments carried out for the CIA by Stanford Research Institute included trying to locate psychically Soviet submarines and describing missile sites. The results are controversial. When government involvement in parapsychology was revealed by an investigative journalist on the *Washington Post*, he also revealed that a report on one part of the work showed that it had failed. Others have argued that it was a qualified success and an independent intelligence expert called in by the CIA to evaluate the project came to the conclusion that it could be used as an adjunct to normal intelligence methods, but was not reliable enough to be used on its own in any serious way.

Military involvement in parapsychological research in America goes back to the 1950s. However, a recent investigation, carried out over two years and costing half a million dollars, on behalf of the American army concluded that there was no evidence that parapsychology was of any practical use, or even any evidence that parapsychological phenomena exist. Obviously, scientists involved in parapsychology challenge these conclusions. But the implications of psi being harnessed for military purposes are so fundamentally worrying that its dismissal by the army has to be regarded with some relief.

The fact that the American army has outwardly rejected psi does not mean that all government funding of psi research for military purposes has dried up. America is not the only country interested in such research. In China, where, culturally and historically, there is a greater acceptance of mysticism and what Westerners would term 'unorthodox' medicine, there is a resurgence of interest in the paranormal and a developing interest in its applications. At Peking's Institute of Space-Medico Engineering, there is a resident psychic who lives with his family in comparative luxury. Zhang Baosheng appears able to move small objects, including insects, from inside sealed containers: the

Chinese are reported to have filmed a pill passing through a glass container. Although, for many years, secrecy surrounded the work that went on in the Soviet Union, it is known that one project attempts to perfect techniques of hypnotising subjects from a distance: a facility which, if fully developed, has horrific military implications. If parapsychology learns to isolate the conditions needed for psi so that the ability can be turned on and off at will by psi stars, society will have to face up to these and other, equally important, implications: the finger on the button might not be under the control of the arm it is attached to.

In the meantime, psi remains fragile – as illustrated by an experiment carried out by the late Anita Gregory, a distinguished psychic researcher, at City University, London, in 1978. The psi star Matthew Manning was asked to interrupt an infra-red beam which was passing between two terminals two feet and six inches apart. Mary Rose Barrington, now a retired solicitor and herself a very experienced researcher, was helping out with the experiment.

'I was in the room with Matthew. He'd just completed a telepathy experiment which had not been a great success, so he was angry. Added to that he was kept waiting to start the next experiment, which increased his anger and, finally, there was an antagonism towards me: for complicated reasons he felt I was against him. So, for all these reasons, he was absolutely seething. I was very tense, too, because I thought he might walk out at any second, refusing to do the experiment. In his temper, he strode across to the beam, glowered and shook his fist at it – and the voltmeter started to go down. I went over and checked that he was not interfering with the equipment. The technician in the gallery was getting very excited because the pen recorder was chattering away.

'I shouted for the others. We had an hour of incredible excitement as the voltmeter went down from 1,000 to 660 for Matthew, although none of the rest of us could affect it in any way. We all went away chatting like mad, planning to do a lot more the following day. Of course, the next day, Matthew wasn't angry, everything was different: we got no effect on the voltmeter. That epitomises the problems of trying to capture the paranormal: it is elusive and unpredictable.'

There are possible pay-offs from parapsychology that do not need to wait for the development of sure-fire psi. At Edinburgh University, Professor Robert Morris and his team have been looking at the relationship between men and machines. Everyone knows of someone who claims to have the uncanny knack of making every electrical gadget they touch break down and others who seem to be able to coax whatever performance they want out of a temperamental car, or a washing machine that's on its last legs. Perhaps nowhere is the difference between the two groups more marked than in their relationship with computers: there are those who take to keyboards and screens like ducks to water, and for whom the computer never seems to go wrong and others who battle to complete even the simplest wordprocessing tasks, with malfunction following malfunction. Are these people, with their dislike of machines, somehow psychically influencing the breakdowns?

Bob Morris's interest was kindled when he worked in the computer science department at Syracuse University, before coming to Edinburgh. So far, the work he and his team have completed there shows no evidence of psychic interference in the running of the computers, either from the 'friendly' or 'unfriendly' groups of users.

'But we've learned more about how people mislead themselves, put themselves in a stereotype. The ones who think they cause machines to go wrong will remember the breakdowns, will attribute the breakdowns to their own malign influence. The people who like the computers and who think they are good with them will treat each breakdown as a purely practical matter, not something that is their fault,' said Professor Morris. 'We also found some physical effects may be caused by their attitude towards the computer. For instance, the person who dislikes working on the computer may drag their feet as they walk towards it, causing a build-up of static electricity. Or they may put off their computer work as long as possible, so that by the time they get around to doing it the equipment has been on for a long time and is tired. We need to do more work before we can come to any firm conclusions either confirming or eliminating psi as a factor in computer malfunctions.'

The work of Richard Wiseman, the parapsychologist magician in the Edinburgh team, also has potential practical pay-offs. The study of how people observe things has implications for police training and knowledge of strategies of deception – how information is fabricated non-verbally – also has significance in fields such as military interrogation and the dissemination of enemy information.

Perhaps the greatest contribution that parapsychology can make to society is to help with the understanding of mental illness. With mental-health statistics running at the alarming rate of one in eight women and one in twelve men needing in-patient treatment for mental problems at some time in their lives, help from whatever source is important. Professor Morris believes that an understanding not only of what is paranormal but of what makes people believe in the paranormal will eventually help psychiatrists to recognize and help with some mental illnesses.

'For instance, people who come up with delusion systems will often incorporate something psychic or parapsychological in there. When some people experience a one-off coincidence between an imagined event and something else that happens externally, they can attribute meaning to it, especially if it happens when they are experiencing emotional ups and downs. If it happens when they are under great stress they may find themselves imagining "they" know what they were thinking.

'Some people respond like good scientists: they form a hypothesis and test it by looking for more coincidences. The more you look for them and the more intelligent and creative you are (and many schizophrenics are creative and intelligent) the more you find to reinforce your hypothesis. Coincidences are out there for the picking. If you find a lot you may notice a pattern and build a framework around it to try to make sense of it.

'There are at least three different hypotheses we can identify which can cause trouble:

- 1 "All these coincidences happen because I have special powers." If you posit special powers that are hard to control, your hypothesis becomes impossible to falsify, you cannot disprove it because your simply ascribe times when it is absent to the fact that your powers were not working properly. You build up a delusion system that attributes psychic ability to yourself and you can get into trouble with that in lots of ways.

- 2 "I don't think I have special mental powers but (perhaps because of a religious upbringing) some other entity does, and I have been singled out for special favour or punishment." Again, you can account for anything within this hypothesis: "they" didn't like you today, or "they" did like you, depending on what happens. This is obviously very damaging.

- 3 If you don't buy any of that you can fall back on good old-fashioned conspiracy theory. "It's only ordinary mortals that are doing this to me but, my goodness, wherever I go it happens, so there must be a lot of them and they're well organized."

'These are three different areas all of which can cause severe mental problems and it may be fairly late by the time they come to outside attention, either directly or indirectly.'

Professor Morris has written a book which he hopes will help people working in mental health identify these delusion systems by setting out what appears at face value to be psychic, but is not.

'I hope it will help to reach people early enough in the day, before the delusion has really got a grip. Because when it gets a grip it can be very hard to shake. A delusion that takes hold of a group – for instance, followers of a cult religion – can take them from a grossly unstructured and unpleasant life and give them a structure that is painfully hard to give up.

'Of course, this does not help the mentally ill who have

active thought disorders which are biologically based. These are the toughest cases to deal with, because they are really scrambling information, misprocessing it all over the place – our world is not their world. I think there is a lot of hope for those who have induced thought disorders, if we can get to them in time. We can help them unpick the experiences that seeded the delusions.'

A greater appreciation of the work of parapsychology would also help psychiatrists who occasionally come up against perfectly sane people who claim to have seen a vision, dreamt the future or been able to pick up information from someone miles away. On the whole, though, individuals who have psychic experiences have them rarely, and recognize that even though they are inexplicable, they are not a sign of incipient madness.

Professor Morris's department, in common with all well-known centres for parapsychology, gets calls from the general public about their 'psychic' experiences, some of which need referral to colleagues in other fields. He is himself an experienced counsellor and his secretary, the first contact when the phone rings, has also done a counselling course. Often the caller only needs a few words over the phone; sometimes they are in need of real medical help. Others, who are having active experiences with ghosts or poltergeists, will be passed on to a branch of the SPR.

The deepening of our understanding of some mental processes is part of the general contribution that parapsychology can make to society, but it is only a by-product of the research that is going on.

Most of all, what all of us want from psychic research are answers to the fundamental questions that, as Hamlet said, 'puzzle the will'. Is there life after death? Are ghosts the spirits of the dead? How do some people create poltergeists? Can we communicate with one another through ESP?

This book does not give answers: nobody has any answers to give. It does, however, seem increasingly likely that, given the high level of intellect and application that is being devoted to the subject, it can only be a matter of time. Whatever time is . . .

Index

Index

Index

Index

Index

Index